ALASKA'S BACKCOUNTRY HIDEAWAYS
Southcentral

ALASKA'S BACKCOUNTRY HIDEAWAYS
Southcentral

by Roberta L. Graham

Pacific Search Press

Pacific Search Press
222 Dexter Avenue North,
    Seattle, Washington 98109
© 1986 by Roberta L. Graham. All rights reserved
Printed in the United States of America

Edited by Margaret Foster-Finan
Designed by Judy Petry
Illustrations and maps by Ayse Gilbert

Cover: *Lodge at Camp Denali with Nugget Pond and
Mount McKinley in the background. Photo by W. A. Cole*

Library of Congress Cataloging-in-Publication Data

Graham, Roberta L.
    Alaska's backcountry hideaways.

    Includes index.
    1. Hotels, taverns, etc. — Alaska — Directories.
I. Title.
TX907.G646   1986   647'.94798   85-32073
ISBN 0-931397-07-3

CONTENTS

ACKNOWLEDGMENTS

There are many people I would like to thank for helping me with this book: Susan Campbell, associate editor of *Outside* magazine, for giving me the final nudge to proceed with the manuscript; the wonderful innkeepers who offered me insight into their reasons for success and a glimpse into their hearts as well; and, photographers R. J. Hayes, John Creed, and Alayne Renee Blickle whose photographs served as the inspiration for several of our illustrations.

I would like to thank especially my partner Craig Medred for his endless hours of support and encouragement, for his endless hours of driving Alaska's highways, for his editorial judgment, his guidance and, most of all, his companionship.

I also would like to thank those friends who offered their much-needed opinions and suggestions; to my constant road companion, *The MILEPOST*®; to Ayse Gilbert, my talented friend who brought a critical perspective to this project and helped bring it to life through her artistic creativity; to the staff at Pacific Search Press for having the foresight to accept what was just an idea, and for their patience in helping to mold that idea into a book; and finally, to Howard Weaver, my friend and former editor who, in his own way, gave me the courage to pursue other dreams.

INTRODUCTION

The seeds for this book were planted in the waning and fast-paced years of the 1970s when, as a writer for a national business magazine, I traveled quite a bit on assignment. I cannot recall what prompted me to begin seeking out quieter places to stay. Perhaps it was the need for respite in an otherwise hectic life. Perhaps it was the enticing New England country vistas—the Berkshire Mountains of Massachusetts, the Casco Bay area of Maine—that lured me into those quaint hideaways.

I remember one trip in particular, scheduled for October just about the time the leaves on New England trees are in their fullest glory. The assignment was to interview developers of the Quincy Market in Boston and then to visit Poland Spring, Maine, to write a story on the secrets of the bottled water company. I remember that trip because at age twenty-six it was my first solo vacation, and the first time my entire agenda consisted of nothing but visiting country inns. It would not be the last of such vacations.

A good friend and colleague, John Jennrich, recommended traveling through the Green Mountains of Vermont. The Quechee gorge area, to be exact. I still have the note he tucked into my pocket. "Quechee gorge outside of White River Junction on Route 4. Bridgewater Woolen Mill." I was supposed to bring back some maple syrup and some woolen sweaters from my trip. To my great disappointment, the Quechee Inn was booked. So instead, I headed southwest into Norman Rockwell country. I had three glorious days by myself to explore the Berkshire country before heading back into Boston and home to Washington, D.C.

While doing the Poland Spring bottled water story, I stayed at the Homewood Inn at Yarmouth, Maine, north of Portland, then headed west toward the Red Lion Inn at Stockbridge, Massachusetts. The second night I visited the Stagecoach Hill Inn in Sheffield, and on my final day, I stopped for lunch at the Village Inn in Lenox before heading back to Boston.

Eight months later, on a summer day in Washington, D.C., so thick with humidity only a refrigerated restaurant provided relief, I lunched with Alaska Gov. Jay Hammond and Robert Clarke, his director of communications for the state. The two of them talked about newspaper reporting in Alaska, reminding me that only four years prior to our conversation the *Anchorage Daily News* had won the Pulitzer Prize Gold Medal for Public Service, the most coveted of all journalistic awards. Between talk of Alaska's bright economic future and the lore of the forty-ninth state, they convinced me that the Greatland was a journalist's dreamland. And I bit.

That fall, instead of heading back to the country inns of the East Coast, a traveling companion and I packed a jeep with only a small portion of our worldly belongings and headed to Alaska. Only once during the two-week drive did we stay at an inn. It seems the travel guides I had stuffed in my map sack previewed only a smattering of lodges and inns of the Rockies. I thought it a shame that no one had ever taken the time to investigate the wonderful backcountry inns and lodges that certainly must be lurking in western Canada and Alaska. We did manage to find a delightful bed-and-breakfast home — a farm actually — in western Alberta. Fall had already settled on the trees, and the air was thick with the smell of approaching winter. While the farmhouse itself was only vaguely reminiscent of New England's inns, the soft feather bed, the room awash in moonlight, and that smell of autumn were all so familiar. I could not know it then, but that was to be my last stay in such a place until I began research for this book.

During the course of the next five years, I was caught in that familiar trap of too much work and too little time for extracurricular activities. I did get out into the country to visit a few of the lodges listed in this book. But it was not until after I left the employment of the *Anchorage Daily News* that I found the time and the inclination to diversify my interests.

Last year, Susan Campbell, one of my editors at *Outside* magazine, asked me to write a piece on accommodations in "Outback" Alaska. I remembered the lack of traveler's guides to such places. Although roadhouses and lodges were the mainstay of Alaska in the early days, no one had ever taken the time to compile a user's guide. Almost before I began reporting the piece for *Outside,* I decided to write that guide to help both tourists and residents find those special places.

ABOUT THE LODGES

I would like to think this book will appeal to people like me who enjoy planning entire vacations around visiting historic, beautiful, and rustic lodges; to people like my friend, Nancy Montgomery, who has the interest and desire to enjoy the backcountry of Alaska but no interest in roughing it; to older folks; to Alaskans who have not yet explored the backcountry; to people in other states who prefer traveling independently but who fear venturing to such a faraway land without the security of an organized tour; and to those who want comfortable lodging while enjoying the wilderness via rafts, skis, and hiking or climbing trips.

Alaska is a bounty of wilderness and outdoor adventure, a land where adventure includes not only the venture itself, but a night's sleep on spiny ground as well. While some of the lodges lean toward the Alaska version of opulence — the hand-hewn logs and extravagant fishing holes — some try to bring a bit of the great outdoors inside. The variety of lodge personalities is part of what enhances Alaska's overall image.

Some of the lodges are accessible only by floatplane or boat, some are old homesteads, some are made of logs, others of clapboard, some are as expensive as three thousand dollars per week per person, others as inexpensive as ten dollars per cabin per night for groups up to eight people.

It must also be noted that Alaska's backcountry lodges, cabins, and roadhouses are not like country inns in other states. I somewhat expected that somewhere in my travels I would find that country inn with tasteful wallpaper, antique brass beds, and a fireplace in every room. I did not. Instead I found that Alaska offers its own brand of quaint, its own brand of charm. I found the beauty, sophistication, and comfort of Kachemak Bay Wilderness Lodge; I discovered the historic and rustic Gakona Lodge & Trading Post with its wonderful ambiance; and, Tokosha Mountain Lodge, probably the one lodge in this book that represents what Alaska was all about in the days of gold mining and fur trapping — adventure, survival, family, beauty.

The lodges, in general, are owned and operated by some of the most hospitable people, of warmest spirit, whom I have ever met. The innkeepers themselves were part of the wonderful finds associated with this book, especially Diane and Mike McBride of Kachemak Bay Wilderness Lodge, Bobbie Jenkin of Quiet Place Lodge, Susan and John Neill of Tokosha Mountain Lodge, Dan and Roberta Ashbrook of Kantishna Roadhouse, and Tom Scanlon of the Fairview Inn.

I also should note that not every lodge in Southcentral Alaska is included in this book. I made a conscious decision to exclude those lodges dedicated exclusively to fishing and hunting and those listed as exclusively bed-and-breakfast accommodations. While a number of the lodges listed in this book do offer guests hunting and fishing options, and some offer prices based on just a bed plus breakfast, most are general family resorts that offer wildlife photography, hiking, berry picking, clamming, canoeing, kayaking, cross-country skiing, snowshoeing, and other activities.

At the end of most sections, I included a list of "Additional Lodging." Though I did not have time to visit them all, I felt these hideaways were worth listing.

About the only common denominator true of every single one of these lodges, I am sorry to say, is the universally bad coffee. I guess it is the price we pay for living in the era of Mr. Coffee and premeasured packages of precious bean.

As for reservations, during the peak summer months accommodations are difficult to get at most of the lodges mentioned in this book, especially those around Denali National Park and Preserve, so it would be wise to make advance reservations. If you plan to visit Kachemak Bay Wilderness Lodge or Camp Denali, for example, reservations may be required months ahead of time. If you want to be more adventurous, jump in the car and make reservations as you go. But do not be disappointed if you are turned away or do not get the exact room you wanted.

Here are some other findings true of most lodges in Alaska:

Most of the lodges will require a deposit to confirm the reservation, but if you cancel, the innkeepers will try to fill the vacancy. If successful, they will refund you your money. If unsuccessful, your deposit is forfeited.

Most lodges, except for the forest service and other rustic cabins, provide meals or have adjoining restaurants. Guests can expect to dine on foods ranging from simple hamburgers to lavish feasts of crab, salmon, clams, sable fish chowder, chocolate cheesecake, and French wine. The meal prices vary from place to place, and some lodges offer a total room-and-board package.

Most lodges prefer cash or traveler's checks only. I have listed preferred form of payment in the "Accommodations" section. Some lodges, however, do accept credit cards. It is best to double-check when making reservations.

Most lodges welcome children, but there are a few that prefer that the little ones stay at home. Most lodges with dining rooms, or those that offer a bed-and-breakfast option, will have booster seats or high chairs and will offer the children crackers or cookies before dinner to placate growling stomachs. However, for parents traveling with infants or small children, most lodges do not have cribs, playpens, potty seats, or toys. Under the "Accommodations" section of each lodge, I have made an effort to point out which lodges offer those special items.

FACTS ABOUT ALASKA

For the uninitiated, Alaska is the largest state in the nation, so large, in fact, the state once had four time zones. Now there are only two. It has the longest coastline of any state, and could hold almost the entire East Coast inside of its borders.

Another "fact of Alaska life" travelers will discover while in search of these lodges is the poor road conditions. Sitting in the Forks Roadhouse one night, I complained about the messy road and the bumpety-bump drive that had almost ripped off the underside of my car. I was telling owner Joe Dul that I had come to the conclusion one must first conquer bad roads in order to get to great places, when one of the guests, Ace Przybyla, offered his own theory. "There's always a pot of gold at the end of the rainbow."

Remember Ace's positive attitude especially when driving the Steese Highway toward Arctic Circle Hot Springs, the Denali Park Road toward the Kantishna Roadhouse or Camp Denali, the road to Hatcher Pass Lodge, the Petersville Road to the Forks Roadhouse, and the Edgerton Highway from Chitina toward the McCarthy Lodge. As Alaska State Trooper Roger Coffey advised me, so will I advise you: stay in the middle of the road, drive the maximum speed and do not stop if you can avoid it.

The scenery along these and most other roads throughout Southcentral Alaska helps to make up for the sometimes tense driving. The grandure of Mount McKinley, the incredible sight of a cow moose with her calf splashing through the Russian River, mine tailings left from excavations done more than sixty years ago, glaciers, fjords, fireweed in the summer, crystal mountaintops in the winter, beautiful Turnagain Arm outside of Anchorage, roadside waterfalls, Liberty Falls near Chitina, Thompson Pass, and the Keystone Canyon just outside of Valdez are all part of what makes these adventures so rare.

Another note of advice, aside from outfitting your car with studded snow tires and carrying chains in the trunk during winter months, you need to come prepared with the proper clothing for the unpredictable Alaska weather.

Of course, it is hard to anticipate what the weather is going to be like anywhere you travel. For that reason most visitors choose the summer months, June through August, which are generally the warmest months with long days of endless sunshine. The summer months also are the only months some of Alaska's backcountry hideaways are open to guests. Come prepared for cool evening temperatures and rainy days, usually in July and August.

A warning to those of you choosing to stay at lodges accessible by air or boat only. Poor weather conditions can sometimes prolong a stay at a lodge by as much as five to six days. And it is possible that the guest might have to absorb some of the expense of the extra days. To avoid the frustration of missed flights or plans gone awry, include some flexible days into your vacation schedule and please do not blame the delay on the innkeepers.

Bring clothing that you can layer. For example, in the winter you might want to don a layer of polypropylene long underwear, topped by a wool shirt or sweater, pile vest or jacket, and a Gore-Tex® wind-resistant jacket. Wool socks are best inside hiking boots or snow pacs.

In the summer months, always plan on cooler evening temperatures. It is best to pack a couple of warm sweaters, pile socks, a pile jacket, a rain coat or Gore-Tex® jacket, and rubber boots or portage pacs made of waterproof leather and Thinsulate® insulation.

According to the National Weather Service, the average Anchorage temperature recorded during July 1985 ranged from fifty-one to sixty-five degrees, and in Fairbanks the average July temperature ranged from fifty-one to seventy-one degrees. Average January temperatures in Anchorage ranged from fifteen to twenty-seven degrees, while the average January temperature in Fairbanks ranged from minus twenty-one to minus three degrees.

The cashier at the Salmon Bake outside of Denali National Park and Preserve asked me to stress, if I stressed nothing else, that warm clothing even during summer months is essential. The average age of the Denali Park visitor is sixty-five years. The cashier said she has seen too many people shivering in polyester suits or light windbreakers, standing sockless in tennis shoes, or wearing sleeveless blouses as they wait for buses or tour groups outside her restaurant.

During the summer months, do not forget the mosquito repellent. And in the winter months, for those of you who drive to the lodges, throw an extra wool blanket in the trunk along with a first-aid kit and flares.

ENCOUNTERING WILDLIFE

Most of the lodges, and especially the forest service cabins, Pirate Lake Cabins, Tokosha Mountain Lodge, and Quiet Place Lodge, are situated in areas abundant with bear and other wildlife. Bear attacks are very uncommon, but do happen. Visitors should be mentally prepared for the possibility of bear encounters.

Here are some tips from *Bear Attacks: Their Causes and Avoidance* written by Stephen Herrero, one of the foremost bear behavior scientists in North America.

The first defense is avoidance, so always maintain a safe perimeter — at least one hundred yards — while in the backcountry. The second defense is noise. Maintain the perimeter and make noise, such as loud conversation with partners, while hiking. If a bear is spotted within that perimeter, travel away from it. But if an encounter with a bear happens, the most important decision is to identify whether the animal is a black or a brown bear. The reason? Each species reacts differently to humans and has different physical capabilities.

Black bears are the smaller of the two, weighing between two and five hundred pounds. They have long snouts like a labrador retriever. Black bears also can be brown in color. Brown bears are much bigger, weighing between four and twelve hundred pounds. Brown bears vary in color from a pale shade of beige to a deep chocolate brown. They have pushed in faces with short snouts like a pig.

If the bear you meet is a black bear, make noise and try to shoo it away. Try to appear bigger and meaner than it is, and do not climb a tree to escape. Black bears climb trees, too. Also, when hiking with small children in black bear country, keep a careful watch on them, as Herrero notes, blackies have a tendency to attack smaller humans.

If the bear you meet is a brown bear, it is best not to make noise. Rather, retreat away from the animal very quietly and very calmly. Do not run. Brown bears cannot climb trees, so you can use that escape if you can climb high enough up to get away from the bear's reach.

If you meet a moose, do not approach the animal because they tend to charge, especially the bull moose during the fall mating season and female moose in the spring when most are with calves. Moose are very aggressive during these two times of the year and will lash out very quickly and violently with front hooves at unwanted intruders.

Most Alaskans who spend a lot of time in the wilderness

carry a 30.06 (or larger) rifle (where legal) and a telephoto lens for long-distance, picture-taking purposes.

If visitors are planning to hike, fish, or hunt while in Alaska, it is best to check with the Alaska Department of Fish and Game for current fishing regulations, areas where fishing and hunting are permitted, seasons, areas where firearms are permitted, and current cost of fishing and hunting licenses.

But mainly, when traveling the backcountry of Alaska in either summer or winter, take time to enjoy the magnificent beauty and the surroundings nature has provided. Listen for the cry of the wolf. Watch for the eagles perched in treetop nests or soaring along the water in search of food. Notice the different species of tundra lichen. Explore the wonders of the coves and bays, the mountain ranges and the rivers. And enjoy your stay.

Dwarf Fireweed

SOUTHERN HIDEAWAYS
Seldovia to Prince William Sound

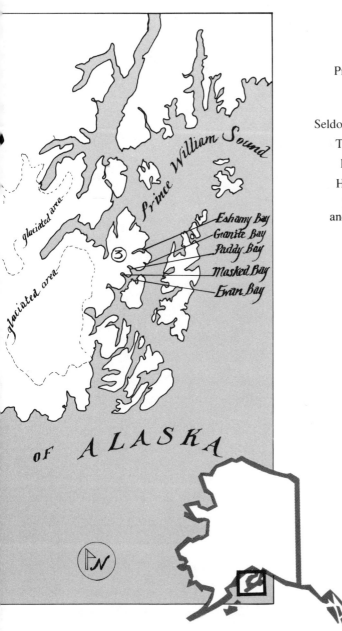

QUIET PLACE LODGE
Halibut Cove

The lush green mountains and the crystal blue water of Halibut Cove provide the setting for Jim and Bobbie Jenkin's Quiet Place Lodge.

"I never get blasé about this place," Bobbie said one afternoon while lounging on the deck of the cove's popular Saltry restaurant. "It's different every day, and I love each of its faces."

We talked about living in the cove where the summer months are fast and hectic with people trying to cram twelve months of outdoor activity into four. There are sixty year-round residents living in Halibut Cove, but during the summer months when the cove becomes a center of tourism, the population doubles.

The Jenkins have owned Quiet Place Lodge since 1982, although Jim has spent most of those weeks in town working as a banker to help finance the growing needs of the lodge. But Bobbie is there everyday and serves as hostess, tour guide, boat operator, maintenance person, and cook. She is so open and hospitable, you begin to feel as if you have known her all of your life.

Her philosophy: always be there if guests want to be entertained, fed, or taken care of, but fade into the background and leave the guests alone if that is what they prefer.

I took the 5:00 P.M. ferry from Homer across Kachemak Bay to Halibut Cove aboard the *Danny J* skippered by Sally Freud and first mate Lisa Greene. Almost all guests of Quiet Place Lodge arrive that way. The trip takes about forty-five minutes — delightful time that can be spent photographing sea otters and puffins and working up an appetite for dinner at the Saltry.

If guests arrive on the ferry, Bobbie suggests eating at the Saltry in order to sample some local bill of fare. The waterfront restaurant offers a sushi-style selection of fresh salmon and halibut

on square, handcrafted plates. It is easily some of the best fresh seafood I have ever eaten. The Poki Salmon is filleted, then salted and cured for twenty-one days. Just before serving, the cubed pieces of salmon are tossed in a teriyaki sauce and sprinkled with scallions. The halibut is marinated for twenty-four hours in a lemon-lime mixture to make a tart ceviche. The sable chowder made from huge chunks of fresh vegetables and halibut, accompanied by thick, crusty homemade bread with sweet butter is almost a meal in itself. I barely had room for the luscious chocolate cheesecake.

After dinner, Bobbie brings her skiff across the cove to retrieve Saltry diners. Her cozy lodge, nestled in the hillside just across the way, is built of simple pine, and each of the four cabins has magnificent views of Halibut Cove.

Recent guests David and Bev Postman describe it as "definitely cozy." "It was pouring down rain the whole day we were there, and we still had a great time," Bev said. "I would give it a AAA rating."

Quiet Place Lodge consists of four cabins and one main lodge that houses the central bath area and a small library. The sauna is tucked into the hillside and offers a relaxing way to spend an evening. Two of the cabins are built into the hillside above the main lodge, and two are right on the dock.

Bobbie calls the cabins rustic, which could be an appropriate term if referring to the fact that the cabins have no running water and no electricity. But I agree with the Postmans in choosing to call them quaint, cozy, and even romantic. This is a great hideaway in the jewellike setting of Halibut Cove.

ACCOMMODATIONS: For reservations or more information write to Jim and Bobbie Jenkin, Quiet Place Lodge, P.O. Box 6474, Halibut Cove, Alaska 99603, or telephone (907) 296-2212. The lodge is open from 31 May to 15 September. Reservations are required at least 4 weeks in advance. A 25 percent deposit is required to confirm reservations. The deposit is fully refunded with cancellation 2 weeks prior to reservation. Quiet Place Lodge accepts cash, traveler's checks, and personal checks only. The lodge offers two packages. The bed and breakfast option is $100 per night for double occupancy. It includes transportation from the public dock in Halibut Cove, the cabin, and a family style breakfast. My morning platter was heaped with scrambled eggs, bacon, toast, and delicious homemade blueberry muffins. A lodge stay option of more than one night is $100 per night per cabin, Monday through Thursday, or $150 per night per cabin Friday through Sunday. Guests receive three meals per day at $30 per person per day. Meals also are available across the cove at the Saltry. The full-service lodge stay includes transportation, use of boats, guided hiking, berry picking, and sight-seeing. Two cabins are on the hillside above the main lodge and 2 are on the waterfront. One waterfront cabin has 2 sets of bunk beds. The other 3 have a double bed and one set of bunk beds. Each cabin has a wood stove, kerosene lantern, fresh bed linens and calico quilts, and a smattering of antiques around the room. The central bath is located in the main lodge. Towels are provided. The lodge also offers a library and fresh coffee at all hours. A separate sauna is located next to the main lodge. Children are welcome, and the Jenkins offer cribs, playpens, potty seats, toys, and other items for infants and young children.

TRAVEL INFORMATION: The lodge is accessible by floatplane, commercial ferry, or private boat. Floatplane transportation to

Halibut Cove can be arranged from Homer. Commercial ferry transportation can be arranged aboard the *Danny J* ferry through Halibut Cove Experiences, P.O. Box 6423, Halibut Cove, Alaska 99603, (907) 235-8110. Round-trip fare is $15 per person. For groups of 4 or more staying a minimum of 4 days, the Jenkins will provide transportation to and from the Homer Airport or the Homer Spit at no extra costs. Also, the Jenkins will take care of ferry and dinner reservations (at the Saltry) for guests if requested. The lodge is located near the public dock at Halibut Cove for guests coming via private boat. Boat tie-ups are free. The Jenkins will meet guests and provide boat transportation to the lodge. Commercial flights to Homer are available from most major Alaska cities. From Anchorage drive the Seward Highway south 90 miles to the Sterling Highway cutoff at Milepost 89.3. Follow the Sterling Highway south to Homer. The drive takes approximately 5 hours.

KACHEMAK BAY
WILDERNESS LODGE
China Poot Bay

There was a swirl of activity going on at the lodge when we arrived aboard our Zodiak Mark II inflatable boat. A boat full of anglers had just returned with the day's catch of king salmon, several other guests were milling about the sun deck of the solarium, and the crew was scurrying to tie up boats and unload equipment. It was a glorious day on Kachemak Bay, and at first I thought the weather and the Fourth of July weekend might have something to do with the hustle and bustle.

Knowing that lodge owners Diane and Mike McBride usually like to keep their guest list limited to between eight and ten people at any one time, I thought the larger number of people out of character for Kachemak Bay Wilderness Lodge.

As it turned out, two days of fog in nearby Homer had grounded a floatplane that was to have taken six of the guests to the McBride's wilderness camp at Chenik. The unpredictable fog had swelled the McBride's guest list to fifteen. Then the three of us arrived relatively unannounced bringing the total to eighteen people.

Still, Diane welcomed us as if we were the only guests there. She managed to settle us in with a cup of steaming coffee while at the same time monitor the weather forecast and flight arrangement and make hamburger patties as part of the evening meal.

"You can never count on the weather to cooperate with your schedule," she smiled.

Kachemak Bay Wilderness Lodge sits tucked away at the end of China Poot Bay across Kachemak Bay from the small fishing hamlet of Homer. The total effect of the entire complex reminds me of a cross between a Bahamian Out Island resort and the Swiss Family Robinson. The main lodge is made of log and sits on pilings at the head of the bay, but the four rough-cut spruce or log guest

cabins are nestled among towering spruce stands. One guest cabin is linked to the main lodge area by a quaint rope bridge twenty-five feet above the sheer rocks and sandy beach.

There is a main barbecue area under a rounded shake roof and a long dock on twenty-foot pilings, which serves as a buffer for the entire lodge complex. There is a sauna, a Jacuzzi, wood stoves in each cabin, a central indoor bathhouse, and flush toilets. Comfort in the midst of the wilderness.

During the past seventeen years as owners of Kachemak Bay Wilderness Lodge, the McBrides have made innkeeping their way of life. Aided by a staff of eight, Diane conducts the nature hikes while Mike organizes the fishing and nature-viewing trips. Their evenings are spent doing things such as playing volleyball on the beach with guests and entertaining the group with Mike's accordion playing. Both never tire of entertaining and socializing even as their guests begin to wilt from the whirlwind of the day's activities.

As we sat in the lodge's cozy kitchen talking with Diane about the summer, my former boss, Kay Fanning, strolled in, baseball cap pulled down around her silver hair. Kay had been the editor and publisher of the *Anchorage Daily News* when I worked there. Now, as the editor of the *Christian Science Monitor,* she makes her home in Boston. But for the past two summers she and husband Mo Mathews have come back to visit Alaska and to vacation at Kachemak Bay Wilderness Lodge. Kay and Mo, along with Frank Turpin, the head of the Alaska Railroad, and former Anchorage Mayor Jack Roderick and their wives, comprised the group of six awaiting the flight to Chenik Wilderness Camp.

Diane interrupted our conversation long enough to contact the flight service in Homer by radio phone. But as she picked up the mike, a plane soared overhead announcing the arrival of the flight to Chenik. Within five minutes, Diane had all six happy passengers on board and on their way to a few days of photo-graphing wildlife and viewing brown bears near the McNeil River State Game Sanctuary.

Chenik Wilderness Camp is a part of the McBride estate and lies in Kamishak Bay in lower Cook Inlet, about one hour southwest from the lodge by floatplane. The camp's tent cabins face active Augustine Island Volcano and have commanding views of Mount Iliamna and Mount Redoubt. Each cabin has a wooden platform, bunk beds handcrafted from local driftwood, sun porches, and outhouses. Chenik also offers a central lodge with a cozy fireplace. But guests to both Chenik and Kachemak Bay should be aware that bad weather in the Homer/Kachemak Bay area can restrict floatplane travel. So guests should include some flexibility in their schedules when visiting either lodge.

After the Chenik guests left and things settled down to a mild roar, we left for a hike along the rugged rain forest trail to Moosehead Point, then up the high cliffs and back to Sandy Beach.

Although meals are usually served family style in the dining room of the main log lodge, that evening guests dined picnic-style at Sandy Beach on freshly caught king salmon, roast turkey, king crab, chowder made from butter clams some of the guests had dug at low tide that morning, homemade breads, potato salad and cole slaw, hotdogs, hamburgers, and imported beers and wines. And for dessert, there was a chocolate swirl cake decorated like the American flag with wild clover flowers patted in place to represent the fifty states.

The next morning we were sipping coffee in the dining room, looking out of the large picture window at the bay and the bird rookeries, and wondering why we had to leave so soon.

ACCOMMODATIONS: For reservations or more information write

to Diane and Mike McBride, Kachemak Bay Wilderness Lodge, P.O. Box 956, Homer, Alaska 99603, or telephone (907) 235-8910. The lodge is open 1 May through 15 December. Chenik Wilderness Camp is open 15 June through 15 August. Reservations are required at least 6 weeks ahead of time. A 50 percent deposit is required to confirm reservations. Full payment is required 45 days before arrival. The deposit is fully refunded with 30 days' notice. Thereafter it is nonrefundable, but may be applied to future booking. Kachemak Bay accepts cash and personal checks only. The rate is $595 per person for a minimum stay of 3 days and 2 nights. A 10-day special package is $2,250 per person for 5 days at Kachemak Bay Wilderness Lodge and 5 days at Chenik Wilderness Camp, including floatplane transportation. All rates include round-trip transportation from Homer to the lodge, all meals and lodging, guide services, and full use of all facilities and equipment. Children are welcome, but currently there are no special items for infants and young children.

TRAVEL INFORMATION: The lodge is accessible by floatplane or boat only. Commercial flights to Homer are available from most major Alaska cities. The McBrides will arrange to meet guests in Homer and take them to the lodge via skiff free of charge. From Anchorage drive the Seward Highway south 90 miles to the Sterling Highway cutoff at Milepost 89.3. Follow the Sterling Highway to Homer. The drive from Anchorage takes approximately 5 hours.

PRINCE WILLIAM SOUND ADVENTURES

Prince William Sound

J im O'Meara is a man of many accomplishments. As an ultralight pilot, he was one of two men who in 1982 flew over the entire 1,049-mile Iditarod Trail during the dead of winter from Anchorage to Nome. But he gave up the ultralights, not because he did not enjoy hanging out of an open cockpit over the rough Alaska terrain, but simply because over the past two years he has developed a new love: Prince William Sound and the seven floating cabins he built there.

And for good reason. The cabins are a great getaway for a week's (or weekend's) worth of sea kayaking, fishing, or just plain relaxing. Jim and I flew out there one beautiful Thursday afternoon along with three other passengers he was ferrying to a fish camp at Main Bay. One of the floatplanes Jim flies from his headquarters on Lake Hood near Anchorage is the rugged *DeHavilland Beaver.* That particular day it was loaded to the ceiling with groceries, baggage, and fishing gear. I rode shotgun in the copilot's seat and could not hear much because of the noise up front. But every once in a while, out of the corner of my eye, I could see Jim shaking his head back and forth with a smile and mumbling, "This is great. I love it."

We flew south from Anchorage for an hour through Portage Pass and over the Chugach Mountains and into Prince William Sound. What a world of difference one hour can make. One would never expect that just beyond the bustling Seward Highway and the ski resort at Alyeska lies the pristine setting of Prince William Sound. We dropped into Main Bay and floated up to the fish camp to drop off our passengers, and then headed to the floating cabin at Paddy Bay.

Jim keeps several boats docked at the floating Paddy Bay camp for his guests' use. He cut the engines and floated up to the

closer side where the caretaker met us and secured the plane. The main portion of the Paddy Bay camp is actually a metal dome in which Jim has put several cots, a dining table, a propane cooking stove, a wood stove, and shelving. Adjacent to the sleeping/cooking quarters on one side is a wonderful cedar sauna and on the other side, a clean outhouse. All three structures sit on the floating dock to complete a very nice if not unusual guest house.

Unlike the Paddy Bay floating camp, the guest house Jim has in Eshamy Bay comes fully equipped with three full-course meals and a cook to prepare them. It is actually a little blue house that sits on pontoons at the head of the bay and looks quite domestic in the midst of the surrounding wilderness.

The other five floating log cabins are in Masked, Ewan, Granite, and Paddy bays. The log cottages are much homier than the metal dome camp and a little more private than the home on pontoons. Each log cabin sleeps four and has a loft that can accommodate two more people. Each of the cabins has the attached sauna and bathroom, two sets of bunk beds (plus futons for the extra guests), propane cook stoves, wood stoves for heat and a wood stove in the sauna, fresh water, and a boat with a motor. These cabins do not have caretakers, and guests do their own cooking.

For the past eleven years, Jim has made his living as a bush pilot and believes that with the right information and equipment, most people prefer to be on their own.

"My business is to provide transportation, information, boats and motors, kayaks, tent camps, and floating cabins so that guests have the opportunity to pursue their interests in their own way. I want to bring Prince William Sound to the attention of others because it's one of the most rugged and beautiful areas in North America. I think people can have a quality experience while keeping to a minimum the impact on the area."

Aside from the cabins, Prince William Sound Adventures offers myriad secluded coves, humpback and killer whales, sea otters, seals, and bears along with over two hundred species of resident and migratory birds.

If you use one of the skiffs for a day of sight-seeing or fishing, do not forget to check the crab or shrimp pots on the way back to your cabin.

ACCOMMODATIONS: For reservations or more information write to Jim O'Meara, Prince William Sound Adventures, P.O. Box 6146, Anchorage, Alaska 99502, or telephone (907) 248-6914. The cabins are open 15 May through 30 September. Reservations are required at least 2 months in advance. A 30 percent deposit per person is required more than 45 days in advance. Full payment must be made 30 days before arrival. Reservations made less than 45 days in advance must be accompanied by full payment. The deposit is fully refunded with written cancellations received more than 30 days prior to arrival, less a $25 per person service fee. Deposits will be forfeited thereafter unless the canceling party fills the space. Prince William Sound Adventures accepts traveler's checks, cash, Visa, and MasterCard. Cabins are rented to groups of at least 4 people but no more than 6. The rates are: $650 per person for a minimum stay of 3 days and 2 nights, and $1050 per person for a maximum stay of 5 days and 4 nights. Rates include round-trip transportation from Lake Hood, a fully equipped cabin, food, linens, towels, use of boats and motors, fuel for motors, life vests and other boating equipment, cooking facilities, and shrimp and crab pots. Guests must bring personal items, liquor, beverages, and fishing license. Children are welcome, but currently there are no special items for infants and young children.

TRAVEL INFORMATION: The cabins are accessible by floatplane or boat only. Transportation via floatplane to cabins or by train to Whittier is included in the cost. If guests go by train, boat transportation from Whittier to cabins also is provided at no additional cost. Prince William Sound Adventures is located on the north shore of Lake Hood near Anchorage International Airport. Follow West Northern Lights Boulevard to the airport. Turn left at the Lake Hood sign and follow the road around the curves in the road until the first available left turn. Follow a short road to intersection. Turn right and go several feet to the road sign for Prince William Sound Adventures. Turn left into the parking lot and drive to lake's edge to Prince William Sound Adventures.

Forget-me-not

BEAR CREEK LODGE
Hope

The forest surrounding Bear Creek Lodge was the color of highly polished copper and brass punctuated by occasional pockets of evergreen. It was mid-September, and some of the leaves had fallen from the branches and drifted upon the pond. Across Turnagain Arm I could see the snowcapped Chugach Mountains, and from anyone's best guess, it looked like the onset of winter. But inside, a glowing wood stove, a fresh pot of coffee, and homemade oatmeal spice cookies let us ignore the chilly day just a little bit longer.

I was sitting in the small cabin of innkeepers Linda and Art Vathke talking about the changes at Bear Creek since they bought it four years ago.

"When we bought this place it was all grown over, and you couldn't even see it from the highway," Art said. From Art's year-by-year account, both he and Linda have put a lot of work into rehabilitating the hand-hewn log guest cabins, putting up new frame cabins, and adding a restaurant. But the setting is so lovely and serene that it was hard for me to imagine it had been any other way.

The tumbling creek, full of golden fins in the summer, runs down from the Kenai Mountains and encircles the lodge. The Vathkes have diverted a sliver of the creek so that it runs under one of the cabins, into their pond, and eventually, down a handcrafted waterfall back into the main stream.

In earlier times, creeks such as this one and nearby Resurrection Creek drew hundreds of gold miners to the small community of Hope. Today, Hope has a population of one hundred people and offers Anchorage residents a pleasant weekend getaway destination for hiking and camping. The thirty-eight-mile-long Resurrection Pass Trail begins in Hope at an elevation of five

hundred feet, climbing to twenty-six hundred feet at Resurrection
Pass. Hikers often begin or end their hike at Bear Creek Lodge.

The lodge sits just off the main road that leads into the old
mining community. Although the road is the only main thoroughfare
into the town, traffic is so scarce that road noise is not a problem at
Bear Creek. A scattering of little log and frame guest cottages, a
small A-frame restaurant, and a wonderful replica of an old log

cache greet guests.

One log cabin and one frame cabin are located next to the pond. The other two guest cabins are located alongside the creek a short way from the pond and the other cabins.

Despite the Vathkes' accomplishments with Bear Creek, Art says there are still some changes they want to make, such as adding more cabins and creating a cross-country ski-trail system on their eighteen acres of leased state land.

In order to finance the lodge's growing needs and expansion, Art has to keep his teaching job in Anchorage. That means every day during the school year, he is up at 5:30 A.M. to ready himself and his plane for the twenty-five-minute, door-to-door commute.

Looking out their window at the quaint, picturesque setting with its small bridge spanning the waterfall, its family of geese wandering the walkways, and the hand-hewn cabins, I had to wonder how Art convinces himself to work in the city.

ACCOMMODATIONS: For reservations or more information write to Art and Linda Vathke, Bear Creek Lodge, Mile 15.9 Hope Highway, Hope, Alaska 99605, or telephone (907) 782-3141. The lodge is open year-round. Reservations are required at least 2 weeks in advance. A 10 percent deposit is required. The deposit is fully refunded with verbal or written cancellation. Bear Creek Lodge accepts MasterCard, Visa, and personal checks. There is no minimum or maximum stay. The rates are: $40 per night for log cabins, $45 per night for frame cabins, and $7.50 for each additional adult. Children are free. Rates include linens, towels, blankets, electric heat, and wood stove; the log cabins offer one double bed and a couch that pulls out into a second bed; the frame cabins have a double bed, sitting area, and separate room with single bed suitable for a small child. A central bath with shower and toilet is in a separate building. Guests need only bring personal items. Rates do not include meals, but Bear Creek Lodge offers meals in its small dining room. Nearby restaurants include the Discovery Cafe and the SeaView Cafe. Call ahead to verify restaurants' hours. Children are welcome, but currently there are no special items for infants or young children.

TRAVEL INFORMATION: The lodge is accessible by plane or car only. There are no commercial flights to Hope, but private or charter planes can land on a nearby airstrip. For flight information, contact Flight Service in Anchorage. Guests needing transportation from the airstrip should notify the Vathkes well ahead of arrival. From Anchorage drive the Seward Highway south to the Hope cutoff at Milepost 56.7. Hope is 15.9 miles north and west. Bear Creek Lodge sits on the right-hand side of the road. The drive takes approximately 2 hours. Along the road to Hope there are many paved turnouts with views of the ocean, bore tides, and mountain sheep.

ADDITIONAL LODGING

Seldovia to Prince William Sound

SELDOVIA ROWING CLUB INN
Seldovia

The Rowing Club is located in the historic Old Boardwalk district of Seldovia, one of the oldest settlements in the Kachemak Bay area. Guests love this old historic home. Most describe it as a very idyllic, peaceful, and charming place. Owner Susan Mumma describes it as a "very romantic place."

"It is the type of place where you would want to spend your honeymoon," she said.

The one guest suite is on the boardwalk level of the home and includes a quaint sitting room, kitchen, living room, private bath, and a deck overlooking Seldovia Bay. The suite is decorated in a nautical theme with pictures and memorabilia of old Seldovia. Situated only one block from the harbor, the Rowing Club is a perfect jumping-off point for exploration of the seaside town.

Before letting her guests venture out, however, Mumma serves up a sumptuous breakfast including the Seldovia Rowing Club's special omelet or blueberry pancakes, poppyseed bread, juices, potatoes, coffee, tea, and other gourmet specialties.

ACCOMMODATIONS: For reservations or more information write to Susan Mumma, Seldovia Rowing Club Inn, Box 41, Seldovia, Alaska 99663, or telephone (907) 234-7614. The inn is open year-round. Reservations are recommended during the summer months. A $20 deposit is required for those booking more than 1 week in advance. The deposit is nonrefundable. The Rowing Club Inn accepts cash and personal checks only. The rates are: $52.25 for double occupancy, and $20.00 for each additional person. Children under 6 are free. Rates include the suite, a hearty breakfast, and transportation to and from the airport. Lunch and dinner are not served, but several restaurants are available in Seldovia. Children are welcome, but currently there are no special items for infants or young children.

TRAVEL INFORMATION: The inn is accessible by plane or ferry only. Flights can be arranged in Homer, and Mumma will provide airport pickup in Seldovia upon request. Ferry transportation is available through the state ferry system and a private ferry operator, Rainbow Tours. The state operates two schedules, a summer schedule between 1 May and 30 September, sailing twice each week, and a winter schedule 1 October through 30 April, sailing once each week. Out-of-state reservations can be made by calling toll free 1-800-544-2251 or at the Homer Ferry Terminal at (907) 235-8449. Rainbow Tours offers daily cruises during the summer months only. For reservations write Rainbow Tours, P.O. Box 1526, Homer, Alaska 99603, or telephone (907) 235-7272. From Anchorage drive south on the Seward Highway for 90 miles to the Sterling Highway cutoff at Milepost 89.3. Follow the Sterling Highway to Homer. The drive takes approximately 5 hours.

THE BOARDWALK HOTEL
Seldovia

Although it is called a hotel, The Boardwalk is really nine rooms of charm situated in the newer section of Seldovia two blocks from the Old Boardwalk. The exterior of rough-cut spruce gives the hotel a rustic appearance but the interior is modern and clean. Each of the nine rooms has a commanding view of either the snowcapped Kenai Mountains or the harbor, each has a private bath and linens, and all rooms are decorated with lots of plants. The lobby has a communal television and telephone and is decorated in an eclectic yet tasteful fashion, including historic photographs of Old Seldovia and owner Annie McKenzie's artwork.

ACCOMMODATIONS: For reservations or more information write to Annie McKenzie, The Boardwalk Hotel, P.O. Box 72, Seldovia, Alaska 99663, or telephone (907) 234-7816. The hotel is open year-round. Reservations are requested. A deposit is not necessary. The Boardwalk accepts cash and personal checks only. The rates are: $54 per night for single occupancy, $59 to $69 per night for double occupancy, and $5 for each additional person. Special rates and weekend packages are offered during the winter months. Children are welcome, and McKenzie has 1 crib available upon request. The Boardwalk Hotel does not provide meals.

TRAVEL INFORMATION: The hotel is accessible by plane or ferry only. Flights can be arranged in Homer, and McKenzie will provide airport pickup in Seldovia upon request. Ferry transportation is available through the state ferry system and a private ferry operator, Rainbow Tours. The state operates two schedules, a summer schedule between 1 May and 30 September, sailing twice each week, and a winter schedule 1 October through 30 April, sailing once each week. Out-of-state reservations can be made by calling toll free 1-800-544-2251 or at the Homer Ferry Terminal at (907) 235-8449. Rainbow Tours offers daily cruises during the summer months only. For reservations write Rainbow Tours, P.O. Box 1526, Homer, Alaska 99603, or telephone (907) 235-7272. From Anchorage drive south on the Seward Highway for 90 miles to the Sterling Highway cutoff at Milepost 89.3. Follow the Sterling Highway to Homer. The drive takes approximately 5 hours.

HALIBUT COVE CABINS
Halibut Cove

It's like camping out in cute little cabins," says Syd Bishop of her Halibut Cove Cabins. Syd and husband Dennis Bishop built the two pine cabins two years ago. Both are nestled in the spruce stands above their Halibut Cove beachfront home. Guests should expect several minutes of fairly vertical hiking to reach the cabins. But the Bishops have installed a pulley system from the beach up the steep slope to the cabins to help guests transport heavy backpacks or other gear.

Syd is a graphic artist and has decorated each of the cabins with touches of her talents. My favorites are the fish prints she does fashioned after the inhabitants of the cove's waters. Fresh, country-style curtains adorn the windows, and a sleeping loft is the perfect place for the kids at night.

The cabins are cozy and a wonderful retreat after a day of kayaking in Kachemak Bay or hiking the nearby Kachemak Bay State Park trails. Both of the cabins are booked well in advance most summer weekends, so early reservations are recommended.

ACCOMMODATIONS: For reservations or more information write to Sydney and Dennis Bishop, Halibut Cove Cabins, P.O. Box 1990, Homer, Alaska 99603, or telephone (907) 296-2214. The cabins are open 31 May through 15 September. Reservations are required at least 2 weeks in advance. A 20 percent deposit is required. The deposit is fully refunded with verbal or written cancellation. Halibut Cove accepts cash and personal checks only. The rates are: $55 for double occupancy, $25 for each additional person, and $5 for each additional child. Rates include water, an electric stove, refrigerator and cooking utensils, transportation from the public dock, guided tours, and boat transportation to hiking trails at Halibut Cove Lagoon or Kachemak Bay State Park. Guests must bring food, sleeping bags, and towels. Children are welcome, and the Bishops have a crib, a playpen, toys, and other items for infants and small children.

TRAVEL INFORMATION: The cabins are accessible by float-plane, ferry, or private boat. Floatplane transportation to Halibut Cove can be arranged from Homer. Commercial ferry reservations can be arranged aboard the *Danny J* ferry through Halibut Cove Experiences, P.O. Box 6423, Halibut Cove, Alaska 99603, or telephone (907) 235-8110. Round-trip fare is $15 per person. The cabins are conveniently located near the public dock in Halibut Cove. Boat tie-ups are free. Bishop will meet guests and provide boat transportation to the cabins. Commercial flights to Homer are available from most major Alaska cities. From Anchorage drive the Seward Highway south 90 miles to the Sterling Highway cutoff at Milepost 89.3. Follow the Sterling Highway south to Homer. The drive takes approximately 5 hours.

HAKKINEN'S HIDEAWAY
Tutka Bay

The hideaway is actually three, 12- by 14-foot cabins situated at the head of Tutka Bay, thirteen nautical miles south of Homer. Owner Anita Hakkinen says there is a beautiful creek on the north end of their Tutka Bay property, and a waterfall that adds a great deal of charm to the landscape.

The wilderness cabins are a perfect retreat after a long day of halibut or salmon fishing, clam digging, hiking, or scuba diving in Kachemak Bay, she says. Guests simply use the cabin instead of camping and cooking out-of-doors.

ACCOMMODATIONS: For reservations or more information write to Ben and Anita Hakkinen, Hakkinen's Hideaway, P.O. Box 1398, Kenai, Alaska 99611, or telephone (907) 283-4248. Cabins are open 1 April through 15 September. Reservations are necessary. Deposit and refund depend on length of stay, but no minimum stay is required. The Hideaway accepts cash and personal checks only. The rate is $35 per night per cabin. Each cabin sleeps 4 to 6 people. Rate includes cabin with bunks, loft, hook ups for gas range, heat, and lights. Guests must bring dishes, utensils, propane for the stove, food, sleeping bags, and linens. Children are welcome, but currently there are no special items for infants or young children.

TRAVEL INFORMATION: The cabins are accessible by floatplane or private boat only. The Hakkinen's provide no transportation from Homer or Seldovia, and boats are not available at the cabins. Floatplane transportation and boat rentals can be arranged in Homer.

KALGIN ISLAND LODGE AND WILDERNESS CABINS
Kalgin Island

Kalgin Island Lodge, one of the premier lodges in the state, offers fly-out sport fishing, wildlife/ wildflower photography, and just plain relaxation. Located thirty-five miles west of Kenai, the island is eighteen miles worth of wonderful wilderness, complete with its own sunbathing walrus and thickets of berry bushes.

Owned by longtime Anchorage residents Charles and Louise Tulin, the lodge is nestled in five acres of land, which overlooks the sandy shore of Packers Creek Lake. The complex consists of a main lodge, five large guest cabins, a health club housing two hot tubs, a sauna, complete workout facility (including aerobics classes), and showers. Guest cabins vary in size, but each offers a private bath with sink and toilet, wood stove, twin beds, and wonderful views of the lake.

The Tulins, original Alaska homesteaders, ventured into the lodge business several years ago because of their substantial holdings of wilderness land.

Says Louise Tulin: "We had all these wilderness properties, and we had been using Kalgin Island for our own purposes for ten years, so we decided to develop the lodge."

Louise, a retired school teacher turned professional property manager, and her husband Charles, a prominent Anchorage attorney, have done more than just "develop" Kalgin Island. They have allowed their piece of wilderness to blossom into a quaint yet lavish facility with minimum impact on the environment. Guests are flown out from the lodge to more than twenty-one fishing spots, yet the Tulins insist on catch-and-release only in some areas and in Packers Creek Lake. They cater to finicky fly fisherman, yet have designed the lodge with connecting decks so that a handicapped person can enjoy the entire resort. They offer three gourmet meals every day, yet cater to the camping spirit with outdoor salmon and halibut barbecues.

The Tulins also have wilderness cabins in two other locations: Red Shirt Lake and Butterfly Lake in the Talkeetna Mountains. Red Shirt Lake is definitely a fishing hole, while Butterfly is simply a weekend getaway.

ACCOMMODATIONS: For reservations or more information write to Kalgin Island Inc., 525 West 3rd Avenue, Suite 311, Anchorage, Alaska 99501, or telephone (907) 272-2158 or toll free 1-800-544-2763 or responding Telex No. 0925131. The lodge is open from June through September. Reservations are required well in advance. A 50 percent deposit is required at the time of reservation. Full payment is required 60 days in advance of arrival. The deposit is nonrefundable, but substitutions are allowed. Kalgin Island Inc. accepts personal and certified checks only. The rate is $3,000 per person for a minimum stay of 6 days and 6 nights. Rate includes round-trip air transportation from Kenai, 4 to 5 guided fly-out fishing trips, all meals, fish packing for transportation home, and unlimited use of the health club. Aside from sport fishing, the lodge offers clamming and beachcombing, hiking, wildlife/wildflower photography, catch-and-release fishing in the lake, and seasonal berry picking. Children are not welcome.

TRAVEL INFORMATION: The lodge is accessible by floatplane or helicopter only. Guests are flown out to Kalgin Island as part of the package price. Flights leave Sunday from Kenai. Arrangements should be made at the time of reservation. From Anchorage drive the Seward Highway south 90 miles to the Sterling Highway cutoff at Milepost 89.3. Follow the Sterling Highway west to Kenai.

GWIN'S LODGE
Cooper Landing

Most people in Southcentral Alaska think of Gwin's as that terrific restaurant near the Resurrection Pass Trail on the way to the Russian and Kenai rivers, the most popular salmon fishing area around. And indeed, it is. But Gwin's offers cabins, too.

The main log lodge, built in 1946 by Pat and Helen Gwin, houses the restaurant offering great hamburgers and sandwiches. The decor is basic. Picnic-style tables with benches covered in thick red vinyl, paned windows that look out onto the highway and trees beyond, a wooden floor, and a dimly lit room give the impression of rustic, warm ambiance.

The roadside cabins are more rustic. Situated on property next to the bustling restaurant, the two duplex-style log buildings each offers two rooms with private baths and double beds. Two other single cabins and two rough-cut spruce bunk houses, each with private bath, comprise the rest of Gwin's lodgings.

When salmon fishing and hiking season roll around, Gwin's becomes one of the most sought out stopovers in Southcentral Alaska.

ACCOMMODATIONS: For more information or reservations write to Ruth and Melvin Beets, Gwin's Lodge, Mile 52, Sterling Highway, Cooper Landing, Alaska 99572, or telephone (907) 595-1266. Reservations should be made well in advance. A 50 percent deposit is required to confirm the reservation. The deposit is fully refunded with written or verbal cancellation. Full payment is required upon arrival. Gwin's accepts MasterCard, Visa, and personal checks only. The rates are: $50 per night per person, and $5 per night for each additional person. Children under 6 are free. Rates include linens, towels, private bath, and heat. Children are welcome, and the restaurant has high chairs and booster seats and offers children's portions on the menu. But there are no other special items available for infants or young children.

TRAVEL INFORMATION: The lodge is accessible by car only. From Anchorage drive south on the Seward Highway 90 miles to the Sterling Highway cutoff at Milepost 89.3. Drive 14 miles to Cooper Landing. Gwin's is on the left-hand side, westbound at Cooper Landing. From Homer drive north 120 miles on the Sterling Highway to Cooper Landing. Gwin's is on the right-hand side eastbound.

CENTRAL HIDEAWAYS
Palmer to Petersville

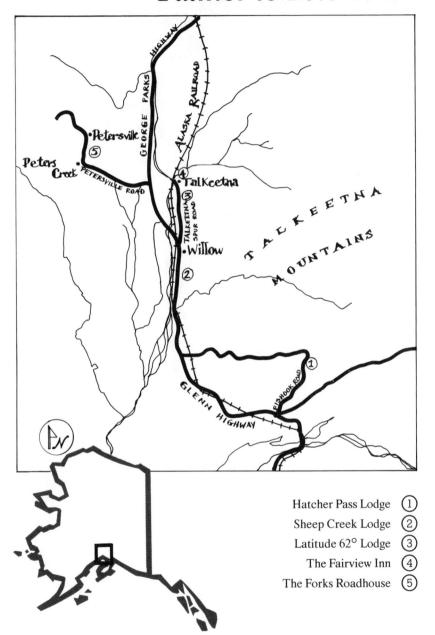

Hatcher Pass Lodge ①
Sheep Creek Lodge ②
Latitude 62° Lodge ③
The Fairview Inn ④
The Forks Roadhouse ⑤

HATCHER PASS LODGE
Hatcher Pass

Hatcher Pass Lodge is many different things to many different people. To some, it is the premier cross-country ski-touring center in the state, to others it is a quaint lodge nestled into the saddle of the breathtaking Talkeetna Mountains just below what is left of historic Independence Mine, still others see it as a great getaway from Anchorage for an evening of imported beer and gourmet dining.

Physically, the lodge is tiny, a thirty-foot-tall and twenty-eight-foot-wide A-frame with a glass front wall that allows guests to look out onto the surrounding valley. A coal-burning stove warms the main room, and large spruce beams loom over a small sitting area with a library, dining tables scattered throughout, and a bar at the back of the room. All guest rooms are above the main room under the eaves of the sloping roof. But the hospitality never stops.

"We used to rent out to groups of skiers who would come up to ski Hatcher Pass. They would bring their own food, sleeping bags, and everything else and just camp out on the floor," Don Svela, one of three managing partners told me. "That worked for a period of time, but it just wasn't making anyone totally happy. Everyone, the skiers and us, wanted more."

Then in the winter of 1980, when the inn at Independence Mine closed for good, the partnership decided to go into the full-time lodge and ski business. It took two years to ready the inn, but in the winter of 1982 Hatcher Pass Lodge opened its doors, as Don put it "as a full-fledged ski-touring center with groomed cross-country ski trails, telemark clinics, races, and everything."

"From the very, very, very first weekend we were open, we've had great response from people," Don said.

As I recall, the opening weekend featured fifty-cent beer and great snow. My partner Craig and I went up for a day of skiing and have been back many times since — in the summer months to poke around the ruins at Independence Mine State Historical Park and enjoy a light lunch at Hatcher Pass, and in the winter to enjoy some of the best cross-country skiing around.

"During the winter months, most of our guests are like you," Don said. "They come from Anchorage, Kenai, Palmer, or Homer, and rooms are booked at least four weeks in advance. But summers are an entirely different ball game. Most people come up to do wildlife or wildflower photography, or to tour Independence Mine [State Historical Park]. I would guess that about 95 percent of our summer guests are from out-of-state," he said. "And at that time of year, rooms are pretty easy to get."

The owners have converted the upstairs loft into four guest rooms, including one dormer-style room. The guest quarters are small, but very cozy and comfortable. If you are a tall person, you will want to make sure you get the outside of the bed in several of the rooms as the eaves slope rather steeply upstairs. Downstairs guests will find a shower and two bathrooms.

The lodge also offers great meals for those whose appetites have been activated by the day's exercise. For breakfast, light eaters should try the fresh fruit salad or the Continental breakfast of fresh fruit and yogurt. Those with heartier appetites might like the Strammer-Max, whole wheat toast topped with two eggs and Havarti cheese served with hashbrowns and coffee. Lunches feature chicken avocado salad, hamburgers, or bratwurst on a bun. Dinners offer a

classy choice of Chicken Parisienne, Scampi Provençale, or Fettuc-
cine. Between meals, the Hatcher Pass bartender can take the chill
off the day with such treats as Mexican Coffee, Hot Buttered Rum,
Mocha-Almond Marnier, Espresso, or Cappuccino.

Travelers who choose to stay at this wonderfully rustic spot
should not forget the sauna over the creek. On many a winter night,
when the moon casts long shadows over freshly fallen snow, a guest
or two has been known to jump from the back porch of the steaming
sauna into the icy waters of the creek below. I have never been able
to figure out whether the howls result from the sheer pleasure of the
sauna-creek combination or the shock of warm bodies meeting icy
waters on a mid-January's night.

ACCOMMODATIONS: For reservations or more information write
to Don Svela, Tom Murphy, or Carl Wurlitzer, Hatcher Pass Lodge,
Box 2655, Palmer, Alaska 99645, or telephone (907) 745-5897. The
lodge is open year-round. During winter months, guests should make
reservations 4 to 6 weeks in advance. Summer visitors require no
advance notice. A 100 percent deposit is required for winter guests
at least 2 weeks prior to arrival; a deposit is not required for summer
guests. The deposit is fully refunded, less $10, with verbal notice at
least 1 week prior to arrival. Hatcher Pass accepts cash and personal
checks only. The winter rate is $60 per night for double occupancy.
Summer rate drops to $50 per night for double occupancy. The rate
for children over 12 years old is $10. Children under 12 years old are
free. Winter rate includes room with linens, towels, and cross-
country trail fee. Summer rate includes room, linens, towels, and
continental breakfast. The lodge has 3 rooms with double beds, and
1 room with a set of bunk beds. The loft has a communal bathroom
with toilet and sink only. Hatcher Pass also offers cross-country ski
lessons: $20 for a half day and $30 for a full day. A daily ski pass is $4.
The sauna is $5 per person. Children are welcome, but currently
there are no special items for infants or young children.

TRAVEL INFORMATION: The lodge is accessible by car only.
From Anchorage drive north 49.5 miles on the Glenn Highway to the
junction of Hatcher Pass (Fishhook-Willow) Road, turn north. The
road leads north and west. The first 5 miles are paved, then turn
to gravel. This road is slippery when wet and can be very muddy
in places. The lodge is at mile 17.5. The road continues over
the 3,886-foot pass and connects with George Parks Highway at
Milepost 71.2. The road also provides access to Independence Mine
State Historical Park.

SHEEP CREEK LODGE
Willow

Emily and Jim Baski own these delightful log cabins along the George Parks Highway. Emily was in the kitchen putting some last-minute touches on the dinner dishes when I sat down at the lunch counter and began eyeing the homemade pies trying to decide between the cherry, the apple, or none at all.

Normally, I would have picked the cherry. But apple is always the better test of whether the pie is authentically homemade. I could not resist the temptation any longer and ordered a piece of the apple. I was just cleaning my plate when Emily joined me at the lunch counter, so I gave her my compliments.

"All of our guests love the pies," she said. But all of the credit really belongs to Grace and Candy Collopy, the "pastry chefs" at this roadside retreat, she told me.

Emily and Jim are brand-new owners of Sheep Creek Lodge. They bought it in March 1985 from Grace and her husband Bucky. The Baskis had worked for Wien Airlines in Anchorage, Emily as a reservationist and Jim as a mechanic. When the airline filed for bankruptcy early in 1985, both of them were put on the unemployment rolls.

"We had been wanting to move out of town for quite some time," Emily said. "When that security blanket with Wien wasn't there anymore, we decided to make the move."

With the enthusiasm of a new parent showing baby's first pictures, Emily showed me around the lodge and the cabins next door. The large log building of the main lodge houses the restaurant, a lunch counter, a gift shop, and the bar.

We had to walk outside to get to the four log cabins. Two of them are fairly small, able to hold only a double bed and private bath. But the other two are larger cabins with a nice loft and room enough for six people, but no shower.

Emily says they have plans to spruce up the cabins, improve and enlarge the cross-country ski trails around their lodge, and institute weekend specials to include dog sledding. Even as is, these cabins are an ideal roadside stopover with great cross-country skiing.

ACCOMMODATIONS: For reservations or more information write to Emily and Jim Baski, Sheep Creek Lodge, Mile 88.2 George Parks Highway, Willow, Alaska 99688, or telephone (907) 495-6227. The lodge is open year-round. Reservations are appreciated but not necessary. A deposit is not required. Sheep Creek accepts Visa, MasterCard, Chevron card, and personal checks. Summer rates are: $50 for cabins with running water and $45 for cabins with no water. Winter rates are $35 for all cabins. Rates are based on double occupancy. Each additional adult is $5. Children are free. Rates include cabin, bed, linens, and heat. Meals are served in the kitchen but are not included in the rate. There are nearby cross-country ski trails for winter use. Special winter ski packages are available. Children are welcome, but currently there are no special items for infants or young children.

Food cache

TRAVEL INFORMATION: The cabins are accessible by car only. From Anchorage drive 88.2 miles north on the George Parks Highway. The lodge is on the right-hand side of the road, northbound, just beyond Willow. From Fairbanks the lodge is located at mile 269.8 on the George Parks Highway.

LATITUDE 62° LODGE
Talkeetna

We like to take reservations as far ahead as our guests like to make them, but reservations here aren't really necessary," innkeeper Jane Milam was telling me. "Especially when we have the mountain climbers, since we're never sure when they are going to get off the mountain."

Jane, of course, was talking about the large numbers of European and Japanese mountain climbers that come every year to try their skill on Mount McKinley, the highest peak in North America. Jane and husband Marv have hosted the international crowd almost from the day they opened for business in 1983.

The Milams are a young couple, pilots by trade, from Anchorage who bought their Talkeetna land in 1976.

"We knew from the day we bought the land that we would build a lodge here," Jane said. It took them seven more years to clear the land, hand peel the logs and build the lodge themselves. But they were determined to flourish in the lodge business.

Almost eight months to the day they opened their doors, a Japanese adventurer named Naomi Uemura came to stay at Latitude 62°. For two weeks he occupied rooms No. 5 and No. 7 in preparation for his solo winter ascent of McKinley, the first time such a feat had ever been attempted. Naomi, a national hero in Japan, much like Charles Lindbergh was in his day or Pete Rose is today, never returned from that attempt. Latitude 62°, Jane, and Marv spent the next two months in the spotlight of the national news media, and long-term hosts to the Japanese climbers who came in an attempt to recover Naomi's body.

In some ways, life for the Milams has never been the same. They are visited regularly by Japanese wanting to see Naomi's last

residence. One of the first things I noticed when I entered through the large wooden door of the lodge was Naomi's picture tacked to the bulletin board inside the door with an inscription that said Naomi will be forever remembered.

But you do not have to be an international adventurer to capture the attention of the innkeepers. The morning I stopped for breakfast, Jane and Marv were preparing for a quick supply flight to Anchorage. Still, they dropped preparations long enough to whip up some of Marv's famous French toast (made with Bailey's Irish Cream), bacon, and freshly brewed coffee, and to spend more than an hour talking about their lovely inn and showing me around.

Imagine the letter T lying flat on its stomach, and you can picture the shape of the lodge. The main lounge and dining room comprise the lateral front portion. Made from hearty Alaska logs that Jane and Marv hand chipped themselves, the lodge embraces you with rustic Alaskan charm the moment you walk in the door. The bar decor is reproduction antique, but the fireplace is real Alaska rock. The dining tables extend from the compact dining room into the bar to handle extra dinner guests.

The eleven guest rooms make up the tail end of the T. Each has a double bed, a private bath, and clean linens. But the rooms have been crafted from traditional construction materials instead of log because, as Jane explained, the high cost and time in building the entire lodge from hand-peeled log proved prohibitive.

I wish I could have visited longer, but Marv had their small airplane waiting on the airstrip all gassed up and ready to go. We exchanged business cards with a promise to talk again soon. I am sure we will.

ACCOMMODATIONS: For reservations or more information write to Jane and Marv Milam, Latitude 62° Lodge, P.O. Box 1478, Talkeetna, Alaska 99676, or telephone (907) 733-2262. The lodge is open year-round. Reservations are appreciated, especially during the climbing season, April through July, but not necessary. A deposit is not required. Latitude 62° accepts cash and personal checks only. The rates are: $55 per night for single occupancy, $60 per night for double occupancy, and $5 for each additional person. Children are free. Rates include bed, linens, and towels. Guests can get meals any time of day, but cost is not included in the rate. A full-service bar is available in the lounge. Children are welcome, but currently there are no special items for infants or young children.

TRAVEL INFORMATION: The lodge is accessible by car, train, or plane. From Anchorage drive the George Parks Highway north to Milepost 98.7. Turn right onto the Talkeetna Spur Road. Latitude 62° Lodge is located at Milepost 14.7 on the right-hand side of the spur road. The drive takes approximately 2.5 hours. From Fairbanks drive the George Parks Highway south approximately 259.3 miles to the Talkeetna Spur Road. The drive takes approximately 5 hours. Transportation is also available via the Alaska Railroad. For reservations or more information call the railroad at (907) 265-2494. In Seattle, Washington, the number is (206) 624-4234. Train reservations should be made 2 weeks prior to travel. There is also a state airport with a 4,000-foot, lighted, gravel runway, and a 1,200-foot village airstrip on Main Street for private pilots or charter flights.

THE FAIRVIEW INN
Talkeetna

My first invitation to visit the Fairview Inn came from owner, Tom Scanlon, nearly five years ago. He and partner Dennis Freeman had just bought the historic building, and Tom thought it appropriate to have some friends up from Anchorage to help celebrate the purchase.

It was late afternoon, about the time the sun sets on an Alaska February day, and the snow was just beginning to fly. We drove past the sign welcoming travelers to Talkeetna and over to the Fairview. Two teams of sled dogs hitched to an empty sled were lounging out in front waiting for their drivers to empty their glasses. No cars drove the main street of the frontier town, only the dog teams and cross-country skiers. From the windows of log cabins and white clapboard buildings along main street came the glow from the evening lamps.

I mention my first impression of Talkeetna because in all of the years hence, it has not changed, and because it is impossible to talk about the Fairview Inn without describing Talkeetna. The two have become somewhat inseparable. I still consider the small town of three hundred and fifty the Alaska version of a Currier & Ives.

During the winter months, the town is a haven for dog mushers, skiers, snowmobilers, and city people trying to escape for a quiet weekend in the country. In the summer months, Talkeetna becomes an international mecca for mountaineers from all over the world seeking to conquer Mount McKinley. The town is the staging area for McKinley climbs, and it is here that groups ready themselves and their equipment for the 20,320-foot ascent. It is from here that they fly to their base camps at the 7,000-foot level of the mountain. And it is here to which they return with tales of adventure, conquest,

and sometimes death or defeat.

In between, Talkeetna revels in its frontier image by hosting an auction of the town's eligible bachelors every December, by hosting the Annual Moose Dropping Festival every July, and the annual Miners Day in May.

The Fairview, a white clapboard building built in 1920 to serve miners and trappers, also has played host to presidents and performers. In 1923, Pres. Warren Harding stayed in one of the six guest rooms above the tavern after driving a gold spike at Nenana to complete construction of the Alaska Railroad. In August 1985, John Denver stopped in to play some music in the tavern while on location for a movie he was filming about Alaska bush pilots.

"I love it here. The old Alaska is still here," Tom said one evening as we sat on stools around the bar in the tavern. And I thought about the many evenings I have spent in this tavern. The evenings filled with fiddle music, guitar playing, card games, singing to jukebox tunes, and dancing across the wooden floor. The evenings spent discussing politics, economics, and the fate of the hand-drawn portraits of local trappers that now line the plaster walls. How right Tom was. This is a wonderful place filled with the spirit of rustic Alaska.

ACCOMMODATIONS: For reservations or more information write to Tom Scanlon or Dennis Freeman, The Fairview Inn, Talkeetna,

Alaska 99676, or telephone (907) 733-2423. Reservations are required, especially during climbing season, April through July. The innkeepers request that guests call the day before arrival to confirm reservations. A deposit is not necessary. The Fairview accepts MasterCard, Visa, and personal checks. The rates are: $20 per night for single occupancy, $25 per night for double occupancy, and $5 for each additional person. All guests share a common bathroom and shower. Rates include room only. Guests should bring towels and personal items. The Fairview does not provide meals. However, guests can dine at several local restaurants including the historic Talkeetna Roadhouse. Freeman and Scanlon also can help plan a variety of outdoor activities including canoeing, rafting, fishing, hiking, Mount McKinley flight-seeing trips, and snowmobiling. Children are welcome, but currently there are no special items for infants or young children. Note: Because the rooms are directly above the tavern, sleeping can be difficult at times.

TRAVEL INFORMATION: The inn is accessible by car, train, or plane. From Anchorage drive the George Parks Highway north to Milepost 98.7. Turn right onto the Talkeetna Spur Road. Talkeetna is approximately 14.5 miles at the end of the road. A sign *Welcome to Beautiful Downtown Talkeetna* lets you know you have arrived. The drive takes approximately 2.5 hours. From Fairbanks drive the George Parks Highway south 259.3 miles to the Talkeetna Spur Road. The drive takes approximately 5 hours. Transportation is also available via the Alaska Railroad. For reservations or more information call the railroad at (907) 265-2494. In Seattle, Washington, the number is (206) 624-4234. Train reservations should be made 2 weeks prior to travel. There is also a state airport with a 4,000-foot, lighted, gravel runway, and a 1,200-foot village airstrip on Main Street for private pilots or charter flights.

THE FORKS ROADHOUSE
Petersville

I had a hard time envisioning one hundred people whooping it up at a New Year's Eve party at the Forks Roadhouse, not because the main room could not handle that many celebrants, but because I was surprised to learn that so many people lived near or visited the foothills on the south side of Mount McKinley.

"The local folks never thought we'd stay more than a year and that was seventeen years ago," owner Joe Dul laughed. Nowadays, the Forks is the center of social activity, as proven by the New Year's Eve bash and dog mushing for the residents of Petersville and others from the city who come out to the country for a weekend of snowmobiling or skiing.

"There must have been fifty snowmobiles parked out there New Year's Eve," said Vera Dul, Joe's wife and chief cook, as she pointed toward the heavy wooden door. "We had a great time."

The Forks takes its name from the main Petersville Road that begins at the George Parks Highway as a wide gravel road and gradually disintegrates into a rutty, meandering mess before it splits into two trails at the roadhouse. From the roadhouse, travel the low road to Peter's Creek for some excellent salmon fishing during summer months, or take the high road into the nearby mountains where gold miners still sift the earth in search of ore.

The Forks Roadhouse, a stopover for those early miners, now provides great meals and comfortable accommodations for those seeking the out-of-the-way rustic inn.

I was sitting on a wooden stool that had been attached to the floor for nearly thirty-five years, watching Joe behind the bar pour beers for Ace, Len, and Fred Przybyla. The group was spending the night before heading out for ten days of moose hunting. They would repeat the overnight stay after the hunt and before heading back into Anchorage, a ritual the Przybylas have carried out for nearly ten years.

I know because Vera pulled down seventeen years worth of dusty guest books from aging shelves above the bar. The Przybylas sat next to me along the bar on those hard wooden stools as we all thumbed through the logs looking for names we recognized. I saw Ace's signature penned in almost every September. I also saw signatures of journalist friends Drex Heikes and David Predeger, and mushers Lavone Barve, Burt Bomhoff, and Ray Reddington, as well as Vera's daughter Shannon Poole, along with hundreds of people I did not know but whose comments revealed that they obviously enjoyed their stay at the Forks.

The rustic log roadhouse is twenty-four feet by thirty-two feet and filled with memorabilia of the days of trapping and mining. "There are buildings that have been here longer than the trappers and miners," Joe informed me. But night had already fallen, and we were too snug to venture outside with a flashlight for a look-see.

Joe recounted how he and Vera have upgraded the lodge since purchasing it in 1968. The upstairs now houses eight guest rooms, each with two beds, and two dormers on either end of the hallway, which sleep eight each. The Forks also offers guests two cabins and an apartment. The rooms are Spartan and without baths, but comfortable.

"Up here you're lucky to get a shower," Vera said. Fortunately, for the dusty road traveler, the Duls have installed two separate baths for male and female guests.

As I slipped beneath the mounds of blankets that night, the full moon shining through the window, I tried to think of what nights at the Forks must have been like. But before I could conjure up any lasting images, I fell soundly off to sleep.

ACCOMMODATIONS: For reservations or more information write to Joe and Vera Dul, The Forks Roadhouse, P.O. Box 154, Trapper Creek, Alaska 99688, or telephone (907) 268-1851. The roadhouse is open year-round. Reservations are appreciated, but in the tradition of a true roadhouse, are not necessary. A deposit is not necessary. The Forks accepts cash only. The rate is $45 per night. Rate includes room, linens, and towels only. Meals are available, but are not included in the price. Breakfast is served until 10:00 A.M., and morning coffee is free. Lunch is served all afternoon but consists mostly of hamburgers. Dinner is served from 5:00 P.M. to 9:00 P.M. Meals are cooked home-style — meaning Vera cooks one dish, and it is served to all dinner guests. A full-service bar also is available

in the dining area. Rates for drinks are separate. Sleigh rides may be available during the winter, but call ahead for more information. Children are welcome, but currently there are no special items for infants or young children.

TRAVEL INFORMATION: The roadhouse is accessible by car or snowmobile only. From Anchorage drive the George Parks Highway north 114.7 miles. Turn left at the sign for Petersville and drive 19 miles to the Forks Roadhouse. The Petersville gravel road is good for the first 13 miles but becomes muddy and very rutty between miles 13 and 15. The last 4 miles are good. Snowmobilers can travel only the Petersville portion of road to the roadhouse. There are commanding views of Mount McKinley.

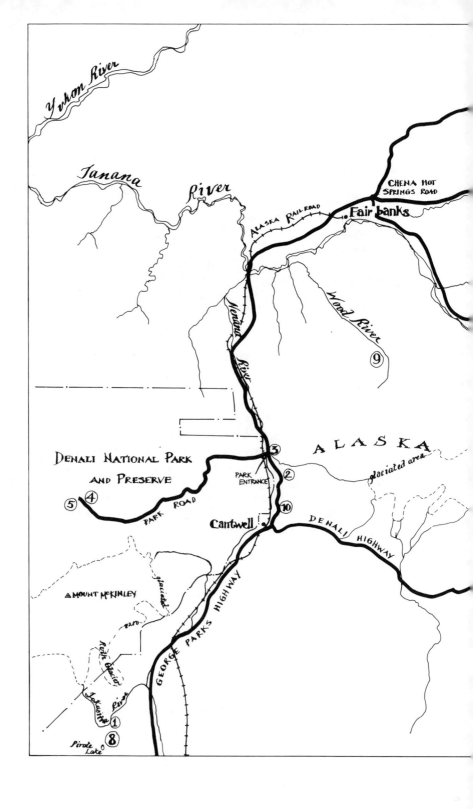

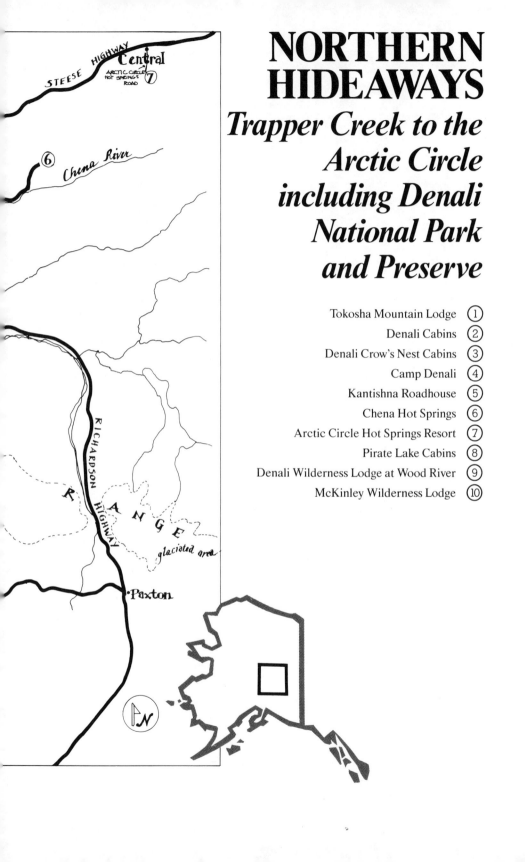

NORTHERN HIDEAWAYS

Trapper Creek to the Arctic Circle including Denali National Park and Preserve

TOKOSHA MOUNTAIN LODGE
Denali National Park and Preserve

The mid-summer rain was warm but came down steadily enough to wash the mascara off the eyelashes and onto my cheeks. Why I had ever decided to put on makeup before going out into the bush, I will never know. Perhaps it was my desire to make a good first impression on my hosts John and Susan Neill. Certainly John was making a good first impression on me, because he chose to ignore the running makeup entirely as he navigated us up the Chulitna River toward his home, our destination, Tokosha Mountain Lodge.

The Chulitna can be treacherous at times, and its channels change hourly. What had been the way into Trapper Creek along the Chulitna just an hour before was now sandbars and exposed trees. John picked his way along the river carefully as we headed into the rain.

On a nice day the view is awesome. The spires of Mount McKinley tower majestically over the Tokosha Mountains (an Indian word meaning treeless). Tokosha Mountain Lodge is a forty-five-minute boat ride or twenty-minute flight from the Trapper Creek/Talkeetna area and is located on the Tokositna River (turn left at the fork where the Chulitna continues to the right).

My stay at the lodge was quite easily one of the most enjoyable I have ever experienced. The Neills — John, Susan, Kenny, and Melissa — are a family of considerable charm, intelligence, and wit. The kids, home-schooled by Susan, are very well-read and cognizant of current affairs, not to mention opinionated when it comes to environmental concerns facing their subsistence way of life.

In the summer months, John guides guests on fishing and hiking trips as well as photography and wildlife viewing excursions. In the winter months the menu changes to include cross-country skiing and dog mushing. Most of what they eat is trapped or hunted by the family, meals are home-cooked over a wood-fueled stove, clothes and toys are handmade.

Over the years John has built and added onto the stockade-style log lodge himself. The result is wonderfully cozy and rustic. Tokosha Mountain Lodge is actually a small kitchen area with thick butcher block cutting tables and a wood-fueled stove, a large main room with huge glass windows that look directly into the face of the Ruth Glacier and Mount McKinley, and one guest bedroom with two sets of bunk beds. The Neills also have a separate guest cabin with bunk beds, a propane heater, and comfortable accommodations for four.

But Tokosha has no electricity, no running water, and no indoor plumbing. During the summer months when the sun sets for only a couple of hours every day, the oil lamps are not lit until 10:00 P.M. or 11:00 P.M., and guests have no problem strolling out to the nearby privy and washing up in the Tokositna. In the winter months, however, Susan says it is quite an adventure.

Despite the inconveniences of wilderness living, Tokosha Mountain Lodge represents what Alaska was all about in the gold rush days — adventure, survival, family, beauty. These qualities remain the standard of life at Tokosha today.

The gentle flame flickers softly against the black bear hide nailed to the log wall in the main lodge. We finished our salmon dinner hours ago. The rain has not stopped, but inside the lodge we feel cozy and safe. Maybe the white wine helps stimulate the inner warmth. We talk about books, the draft management plan the

National Park Service has just released for Denali National Park, and other economic issues.

Susan and Kenny say they like science fiction and fantasy books with a little Arthurian legend thrown in. John says he highly disapproves of the draft plan. All three talk at the same time, and ask questions at the same time. Melissa has long since disappeared. I am somewhat grateful to be juggling only three conversations instead of four. I guess it is a symptom of bush life. A guest at Tokosha is a chance for the Neills to solicit a different perspective on issues and life in general. It is well past midnight when we say goodnight. Fog has settled over the Tokositna. John says he hopes it will lift by morning. He does not want to navigate the fickle Chulitna in heavy fog.

ACCOMMODATIONS: For reservations or information write to John and Susan Neill, Tokosha Mountain Lodge, Box 13-188, Trapper Creek, Alaska 99638, or telephone (907) 733-2821. The Neills have a radio phone and getting a connection may require patience. The lodge is open year-round. Reservations are required. A 25 percent deposit must be received 30 days in advance. The deposit is non-refundable. Tokosha Mountain Lodge accepts cash and traveler's checks only. Summer rates are: $465 per person for a minimum stay of 2 nights and 3 days and $1,125 per person for a maximum stay of 7 days and 6 nights. Rates include round-trip air transportation from Talkeetna (add $160 if trip originates in Anchorage), all meals, lodging, and guided activities. Winter rates are: $395 per person for 3-day, 2-night dog sled trip, and $325 per person for a 3-day, 2-night cross-country ski trip. Rates include meals, lodging, guided ski trips or dog teams. Winter guests should bring their own sleeping bags, warm clothing, and ski equipment. Summer guests should bring rubber boots, raincoat and rain pants, and fishing license. Fishing tackle provided. Any additional lodging costs due to inclement weather will be shared by the clients at the lodge at $90 per day. Children are welcome, but currently there are no special items for infants or young children.

TRAVEL INFORMATION: Tokosha Mountain Lodge is accessible by floatplane, river boat, dog sled, and skis only. The Neills will make all travel arrangements for guests from either Anchorage or Talkeetna. The travel cost is included in the package price.

DENALI CABINS
Denali National Park and Preserve

W e consider ourselves to be more than just innkeepers. We want to be remembered by our guests as experience makers," said Gary Kroll, owner of the Denali Cabins. "When my wife and I go somewhere, we like to be treated special. Sometimes we don't get the special treatment, so we know what it's like."

"In our case, I think people want the wilderness, but they want it on their own terms. So we help them enjoy their trip as much as possible by giving them nice cabins in the wilderness and very special treatment," he said.

Gary and Danae obviously are doing something right because last year they took ten thousand people rafting with Denali Raft Adventures, their subsidiary business at Denali Park, and housed more visitors to the park than in any other previous summer season.

Gary was a state park ranger based in Tok and then a park supervisor before starting the rafting business. He built the first nine cabins on the Nenana River just outside of Denali National Park and Preserve to house his rafting customers. That was in 1981. Now Gary and Danae have thirty-five more cedar Pan Abode cabins just across the George Parks Highway from the original nine, and seven miles south of the park entrance. The cabins are not rustic by any means. Each cabin has two double beds, warm blankets, clean linens, and electric heat. The Krolls also offer their guests the option of reserving a larger log suite, the McKinley Suite, with its own private sitting room and larger bedrooms.

Instead of private baths in each cabin, the Krolls have opted to build four separate Pan Abode bathhouses and place them in convenient locations throughout the cabin park. Each central shower

house is two-sided—one side for women and the other for men. Each is as comfortable as your bathroom at home having two showers, two sinks, and two toilets. And just around the corner, in the middle of the park, sits an eight-foot-wide outdoor hot tub.

"Sometimes I walk the property looking for little things to improve upon," Gary said as we toured the grounds, "and I remember the first time I walked the property. I thought 'Gee, it's kinda plain but maybe we can make something of it.'"

ACCOMMODATIONS: For reservations or more information write to Gary and Danae Kroll, Denali Cabins, Box 427, Denali National Park and Preserve, Alaska 99755, or telephone (907) 683-2643 after 1 May. Cabins are open from 1 May through 15 September. Reservations are required at least 2 months prior to 1 May. A $60 deposit is required to confirm reservations. Consult owners on deposit refund and type of payment preferred. Full payment is due upon departure. The rates are: $60 per night per cabin. Cabins accommodate up to 4 people. Rate includes pickup from Denali airstrip or the railroad station in the park, the cabin, use of hot tub, linens, and towels. Cooking is not allowed in the cabins, but a dozen barbecue pits are available on the grounds. There are several restaurants located nearby. The Krolls also offer the Nenana River raft trips at $25 per person for a 12-mile trip or $42 per person for the 22-mile trip. Wildlife tours and horseback rides also are available nearby. Children are welcome, and cribs or playpens are available for infants and young children upon request.

TRAVEL INFORMATION: The cabins are accessible by car, train, or plane. From Anchorage drive the George Parks Highway north to Milepost 231. The drive takes approximately 5 hours. From Fairbanks drive the George Parks Highway south 120 miles to the cabins. The drive takes approximately 2.5 hours. Transportation also is available via the Alaska Railroad. For reservations or more information contact the railroad at (907) 265-2494. In Seattle, Washington, the number is (206) 624-4234. Train reservations should be made 2 weeks prior to travel. An airstrip is located within the park for private pilots or charter flights.

Shooting Star

DENALI CROW'S NEST CABINS
Denali National Park and Preserve

When I first saw the Crow's Nest cabins from Denali's Park Road, I was struck by how much they reminded me of a Swiss alpine village. It was dusk on a relatively rainy and cold evening. Still, the cabin porch lights twinkled in the evening glow in such an inviting way that I already felt warmed just thinking about settling in. The log cabins are built into the side of Sugar Loaf Mountain and overlook the George Parks Highway across to Horseshoe Lake at the entrance to Denali National Park and Preserve.

"We want people to say 'Hey, what in the heck is that? Let's go up and see,'" said owner Mike Crofoot. He and wife Carol not only built the entire cabin complex, complete with hot tubs, but run the cabins, the raft trips, and horseback riding adventures all season as well. In all, the Crofoots have sixteen small A-frame log cabins with red metal roofs on three ascending tiers. All cabins on each tier are connected by a series of spruce boardwalks. The second and third levels each has a central bath, one for women and one for men, and the third level houses two hot tubs. Mike plans to add a prow-front restaurant to the third level and perhaps more cabins. But given the quality of his existing establishment, Denali Crow's Nest Cabins are easily the nicest of those along the road outside the park.

I sat one evening on the lower deck waiting for Mike to take care of a group of guests preparing for a raft trip, and chuckled to myself over how much the atmosphere on the deck reminded me of a New York sidewalk café. Large red, white, and blue table umbrellas with the "Bolla" insignia embossed on them were centered above thick pine picnic tables. Across the way, near where I waited, white, wire lawn furniture graced the deck. Yet snowshoes, the Alaska

symbol of adventure and daring, were tacked onto the side of the nearest log cabin sitting just next to the Bolla umbrella.

"People sit outside a lot and get to know each other," Mike said. "I guess there's a real social aspect to it."

Inside, the cabins are cozy and private. Each is situated so that it looks out onto Horseshoe Lake, not into the neighboring cabin. Each has a double bed, warm blankets and linens, a writing table, and small lamps.

Aside from great hospitality and comfort, Denali Crow's Nest also offers great deals on white-water raft trips. "It's actually right at your doorstep here, because we overlook the Nenana River," Mike said. "After a day of rafting we pick you up and deliver you straight to the hot tubs."

ACCOMMODATIONS: For reservations or more information write to Carol and Mike Crofoot, Denali Crow's Nest Cabins, P.O. Box 700, Denali National Park and Preserve, Alaska 99755, or call (907) 683-2723 or (907) 683-2321. The cabins are open 31 May through 15 September. Reservations are required at least 2 months in advance. A $65 deposit confirms reservation. The deposit is fully refunded with cancellation at least 7 days prior to reservation date. After that time, a full refund is issued only if the vacancy is filled. Consult owners on type of payment preferred. The rate is $65 per night for a cabin. Cabins sleep 4 people. Rate includes linens, towels, use of the hot tub, and round-trip transportation from the railroad station in the park. There are no meals and cooking is not allowed in the cabins. Cabins are located within a short walk of The Denali Salmon Bake. Several other good restaurants are within walking distance. The Crofoots also can arrange raft trips and horseback riding adventures. Children are welcome, but currently there are no special items for infants or young children.

TRAVEL INFORMATION: The cabins are accessible by car, train, and plane. From Anchorage drive the George Parks Highway north to Milepost 239. The drive takes approximately 5 hours. From Fairbanks drive the George Parks Highway south 120 miles to the cabins. The drive takes approximately 2.5 hours. Transportation also is available via the Alaska Railroad. For reservations or more information contact the railroad at (907) 265-2494. In Seattle, Washington, the number is (206) 624-4234. Train reservations should be made 2 weeks prior to travel. An airstrip is located within the park for private pilots or charter flights.

CAMP DENALI
Denali National Park and Preserve

Wally and Jerri Cole will be the first to tell you that Camp Denali is not for everyone. The environmental retreat is specifically geared for those who want to learn more about Denali's fauna and flora.

"This is really for natural history tour groups and people interested in learning more about the natural history of the area," Wally said. "I would say that about 75 percent of our guests are natural history buffs and the other 25 percent are simply vacationers."

Jerri added: "But we try to program the whole experience here so that those 25 percent don't feel left out. We do try to open the eyes of those other 25 percent to the wonders of the wildflowers and the surrounding beauty of the area."

It is no wonder the Coles want to share as much of their wilderness life-style with guests as possible. The camp, consisting of eighteen log guest cabins, the main lodge, a dining hall, a greenhouse where all the camp's fresh vegetables are grown, central bathhouses, and a darkroom, lies twenty-eight miles north as the crow flies from Mount McKinley at the end of the only road into Denali Park.

From where we sat, I could see the Kantishna foothills, but Mount McKinley was veiled by a low bank of gray clouds. "What kind of a view do you get of McKinley from here?" I asked. Jerri pulled out a book entitled *A Tourist Guide to Mount McKinley,* by Bradford Washburn and opened to the two-page color spread in the middle. I had seen this picture at least a million times, but had always thought it had been taken from Wonder Lake. In fact, the Washburn photo was taken about six feet away from in front of Nugget Pond outside the lodge window, Jerri told me.

In his account of the park road, Washburn wrote: "The view

of Mount McKinley across Nugget Pond from Camp Denali is unforgettable, particularly at sunset."

The minimum stay at Camp Denali is four nights and five days, and the Coles definitely make it worth your while. Among the daily activities from which a guest can choose are hiking, canoeing, white-water rafting, natural history and photography trips (the Coles have a complete darkroom for development of those wonderful photographs), and what they call the "fly-hike."

Those who choose the fly-hike can elect either a six-minute flight to a ridge top west of Camp Denali followed by a six-mile hike to a preordained pickup site, or a longer flight-seeing trip around Mount McKinley to the 7,300-foot Kahiltna Glacier followed by the same six-mile hike back to the pickup site.

Jerri and Wally have lived and worked in this part of the country for a long time, and they are understandably enthusiastic about the wildlife and the lichen. But they are hardly rigid about how guests spend their time.

We were sitting in the Camp Denali lodge amongst the soft strains of Pachebel's Canon in D Major, bound volumes of literature about Alaska's Arctic, exploration and adventure, and an elaborate insect collection under glass. In the middle of the room a guest stoked glowing logs in the open fireplace. Several others had opted to forgo the afternoon hike in favor of reading books in the lodge.

"Age or athletic ability is not a qualification for a stay with us," Jerri said. "We have had people in their seventies who hiked the trails and ridges, and we have had a few in their thirties who found Camp too rustic and unsophisticated for their tastes."

While guests need not be capable of climbing Mount McKinley, they must be able to walk over the tundra from guest cabins to the lodge, dining hall, and bath facilities. The walks are not far and are invigorating for those who have been sedentary. Besides, the great home-cooked meals make working up the appetite worth the effort.

In fact, a previous visitor said Camp Denali "provides guests with a chance to live in the wild while enjoying a few of civilization's greatest pleasures, among them home-baked bread and good companionship."

One of my favorite things about Camp Denali, I must admit, is the ranch gate at the entrance to the Camp Denali road. *Camp Denali. Wilderness Vacation Retreat. Registered Guests Only. Phone before Coming up Hill,* it says. Do not be intimidated. Just pick up the phone in the green box to the left of the sign and tell whomever answers that you are on your way up about to enjoy one of the best wilderness experiences of a lifetime.

ACCOMMODATIONS: For reservations or more information write to Wally and Jerri Cole, Camp Denali, P.O. Box 67, Denali National Park and Preserve, Alaska 99755, or telephone during summer months (907) 683-2290, and during winter months (907) 683-2302. The cabins are open May through early September. Space is often limited so early reservations are advised. A $200 deposit per person is required to confirm reservations. The deposit is fully refunded if reservations are cancelled by 1 April. Camp Denali accepts cash and personal checks only. The rates are: $650 per adult and $488

per child for a minimum stay of 5 days and 4 nights. Camp Denali offers a 10 percent reduction for stays over 5 nights or if 3 or more from the same family occupy the same cabin. Each cabin sleeps 4. Rates include all lodging, meals, round-trip transportation from the railroad station in the park, guided hiking, and other activities.

Camp Denali also offers the Hawk's Nest housekeeping cabin, located 1 mile from the main camp, which sleeps 4 to 6 people and is suited to a more independent vacation. The cabin comes complete with wood stove, propane range, propane lights, all utensils and bedding, fuel, and cold water. Rates are $125 per day for up to 4 guests and $150 per day for up to 6 guests for a minimum stay of 4 nights and 5 days. Meals are extra. Breakfast or lunch at Camp Denali is $9 per person, dinner is $20 per person. The deposit policy is the same as for regular Camp Denali cabins. Children are welcome, but currently there are no special items for infants or young children. Camp Denali also offers no babysitting service, and its programs are geared for family participation.

TRAVEL INFORMATION: The camp is accessible by car, bus, or plane. From Anchorage drive the George Parks Highway north 237 miles to the park entrance. The drive takes approximately 5 hours. From Fairbanks drive the George Parks Highway south 120 miles to the park entrance. The drive takes approximately 2.5 hours. Transportation to the park also is available via the Alaska Railroad. For

reservations and more information contact the railroad at (907) 265-2494. In Seattle, Washington, the number is (206) 624-4234. Train reservations should be made 2 weeks prior to travel. From the park entrance, guests can drive the 90 miles to Camp Denali via the Denali Park Road or take the free shuttle bus operated by the camp. Independent travelers must obtain a road pass from the Denali Ranger Station at the park entrance. When driving the road be aware of the 35-mile-per-hour speed limit and the park's requirement to pull over for oncoming tour buses. Guests should be aware of the narrow and winding stretch of road beginning at Mile 44, the east fork bridge over the Toklat River. From there, the road will climb steadily upward to Polychrome Pass, elevation 3,500 feet. The road here is extremely narrow. Switchbacks wind upward, and the going can be tense. Expect about 5 minutes of nerve-racking driving. From Polychrome Pass to the Eielson Visitor's Center, views of Mount McKinley are spectacular, and the road is good. The lodge bus will stop often for guests to view or photograph wildlife. A one-way trip takes between 4 and 5 hours. Abundant wildlife can be seen along the way. A private airstrip is available at Kantishna for private pilots or charter flights.

KANTISHNA ROADHOUSE
Denali National Park and Preserve

I was eating supper when the tour group arrived. Supper at Kantishna is served buffet-style, and seating is family style. The buffet line wrapped around my table, so I had a chance to hear snippets of conversation from those who had come from as far away as New Jersey, California, and Florida.

"I really wanted an Alaskan adventure," said one from the group as she shuffled past, "and this is definitely it."

From the tone of her voice and the emphasis put on certain words, it was clear that she made the statement half out of anxiety and half out of anticipation. As it turned out, no one in the tour group had been given any information about Kantishna or its accommodations until the day of their visit. The tent cabins and rustic environment of the old mining community had, obviously, taken them by surprise. But undaunted, the tourists pressed on, filling their dinner plates to overload capacity and settling in for a wonderful stay.

Situated at the end of the ninety-one and one-half-mile dirt road into the heart of Denali National Park and Preserve, Kantishna (population four) was a boom town in 1906. The original roadhouse was built to service, feed, and house the area's five thousand placer miners. But all that is gone now. The old roadhouse still stands awaiting rehabilitation, and the remaining miners are themselves a threatened breed.

Dan and Roberta Ashbrook, two of the town's four residents, have owned and operated the new Kantishna Roadhouse since 1983 when they put up the tent cabins for a group of Anchorage geologists. But they are by no means newcomers to the area. Dan has homesteaded at Kantishna for more than twenty-five years. He is also a bush pilot, a trapper, and a musher. White-bearded and robust

with clear blue eyes and a kind soul, Dan is virtually a caricature of the typical Alaska bush male. Berta is younger, equally as compassionate and kind, strong of heart, and a wealth of information about the area. During the off-season at Kantishna, if there is one, Berta sews fur hats and vests from the martens (sable) that Dan traps. During the summer months, she helps in the kitchen, serves as a tour guide and keeps Kantishna on course.

Between them, Dan and Berta have molded the roadhouse into a one-of-a-kind place. Guests have the feeling of being out in the middle of the wilderness but are surrounded by elements of civilization. Most stay in tent cabins of white tarp pulled over pine frames that were originally put up to house the geologists, but shower in nice central bath areas. Guests sleep on cots with thick woolen blankets pulled up to ward off the late summer chill and can fire up propane heaters for additional comfort. Oil lamps light the tent cabins. Hungry visitors can wander into the kitchen day or night for a piece of leftover apple pie or oatmeal cake and fresh coffee.

Both Dan and Berta take the time to tell their guests about

the community and its long history. They pamper them, they joke with, and they cajole them. They show overwhelming concern for their comfort and enjoyment.

After a hearty dinner highlighted by thick pork chops, home-made vegetable soup, slices of corn bread still moist and hot from the oven, and a dessert choice between apple pie with raisins or oatmeal cake with cream cheese frosting, some of us continued our dinner conversation around the pine picnic-style tables. I sat talking with Arlene and Don Sackman of Miami, Florida.

We were listening to the music of EmmyLou Harris and Jerry Jeff Walker played on the roadhouse's compact digital disc unit and marveling at how easily the old embraces the new. The Sackmans wanted to learn all they could about Alaska to augment the short amount of time they had to spend here. They had flown into Fairbanks two days ago to join the tour group. From Kantishna they would go to Anchorage for two days, then catch a cruise ship to Juneau and back to Seattle and the lower forty-eight.

We talked about the tense drive along the ninety-one miles of Park Road, the ambiance of Kantishna and other places that we had visited. The Alaska trip had been Arlene's idea. She said Don's idea of roughing it was staying anywhere but the Ritz in London. We laughed realizing that if the Ritz could have an alter ego, Kantishna would be it.

In addition to tour groups and those who wander in off the road, the roadhouse is also used by local miners. The pub is open to them as is the dining room. And they definitely provide a bit of local color.

As we chatted, Paul Wieler, part owner and operator of Gold King Miners in the Kantishna Mountains, wandered over and joined in the conversation. When he discovered that Arlene taught school, he begged for a reading of Robert Service's most famous poem, "The Shooting of Dan McGrew." But Arlene refused, and the conversation eventually rolled around to talk of gold.

Just like it must have been in the days of yore, Paul talked about the recent luck of his neighbor in finding a nine-ounce gold nugget. He pulled out his half-ounce nugget to show, then a spice jar full of what looked to us to be dirty brown pebbles.

"Just add a little water, swirl it around, and there is no doubt that this is gold," he said, slapping the jar of Kantishna gold down next to the book of Service poems. I contemplated whether I had been caught in some sort of time warp when the volume on the digital disc player was turned up, and the voice of Jerry Jeff Walker convinced me otherwise.

A travel agent from Los Angeles joined our late-night conversation, as did a woman from Anchorage who journeys to Kantishna regularly, "just to get away from town," she said. Guests were beginning to drift back to their tent cabins in preparation for the next day's hike and wildlife tour. Because Berta helps prepare the morning meal, she had retired early, but Dan was still up and making the rounds to ensure that all of his guests were settled, comfortable, and enjoying themselves.

ACCOMMODATIONS: For reservations or more information write to Dan and Roberta Ashbrook, Kantishna Roadhouse, Box 397, Denali National Park and Preserve, Kantishna, Alaska 99755, or telephone (907) 733-2535. The roadhouse is open year-round. Reservations are not required for individual travelers or small groups. Larger groups must make reservations well ahead of travel time, as Kantishna also houses tour groups. A deposit is required for larger groups. Kantishna accepts cash or traveler's checks only. The rate is $100 per night, per person. Rate includes cabin, all meals, linens, and shower. Summer package rates, June through September, are $295 per person for 3 days and 2 nights. Rate includes round-trip bus transportation from the railroad station in the park, cabin, linens, towels, meals, and guided hikes through the gold country. Rate for a one-day flight-seeing tour is $225 per person, including round-trip air transportation to Kantishna via Mount McKinley, gold panning, and a homecooked lunch. Rate for spring holiday, 1 March through 15 April, is $1,100 per person for 1 week. Rate includes round-trip transportation from the railroad station in the park, cabin, linens, towels, meals, and a week of cross-country skiing and dog mushing across the frozen snow beneath Mount McKinley. Guided overnight trips into the mountain passes of the Alaska Range or to a remote trapline cabin are also available. When making reservations for any of the packages, be sure to request either trapper cabins or tent cabins. Children are welcome, but currently there are no special items for infants or young children.

TRAVEL INFORMATION: Kantishna is accessible by car or plane only. From Anchorage drive the George Parks Highway north 237 miles to the park entrance. The drive takes approximately 5 hours. From Fairbanks drive the George Parks Highway south 120 miles to the park entrance. The drive takes approximately 2.5 hours. Transportation to the park also is available via the Alaska Railroad. For reservations and more information contact the railroad at (907) 265-2494. In Seattle, Washington, the number is (206) 624-4234. Train reservations should be made 2 weeks prior to travel. From the park entrance drive the 92 miles to Kantishna via the Denali Park

Road. Independent travelers must obtain a road pass from the Denali Ranger Station at the park entrance. When driving the road be aware of the 35-mile-per-hour speed limit and the park's requirement to pull over for oncoming tour buses. Guests should be aware of the narrow and winding stretch of road beginning at Mile 44, the east fork bridge over the Toklat River. From there, the road will climb steadily upward to Polychrome Pass, elevation 3,500 feet. The road here is extremely narrow. Switchbacks wind upward and the going can get tense. Expect about 5 minutes of nerve-racking driving. From Polychrome Pass to the Eielson Visitor's Center, views of Mount McKinley are spectacular, and the road is good. The lodge bus will stop often for guests to view or photograph wildlife. A one-way trip takes between 4 and 5 hours. Abundant wildlife can be seen along the way. A private airstrip is available at Kantishna for private pilots or charter flights.

Wild Rose

CHENA HOT SPRINGS
Fairbanks

I had heard about Chena Hot Springs for years from friends and Fairbanksians who had enjoyed the hot mineral pools and the warm inviting ambiance of the resort. I had even made plans several times to visit, but at the last minute the agenda would change, and I would have to cancel my plans. When I finally did visit, I was completely surprised by what I found. I had not expected Victorian decor throughout the traditional Alaska log lodge, extending even into the many executive meeting rooms. I had not expected the acres of groomed lawn and the cabin-lined sidewalks. I had not expected to find veteran Iditarod dog musher Jan Masik in charge.

Jan, who has raced his dog team the 1,049 miles from Anchorage to Nome many a time, brings an element of outdoor adventure to an otherwise stately resort. Although most guests still travel to Chena to take advantage of the mineral pools, the Czechoslovakian-born innkeeper has incorporated cross-country ski trails, dog mushing, and some downhill skiing into the resort's winter menu of activities. Guests spend the summer months hiking in the nearby mountains and swimming in the indoor pools of mineral water.

For breakfast, my partner Craig and I seated ourselves at a table with a nice view of the surrounding grounds. We expected to enjoy the early morning sunshine after several days of constant rain. Adding to the nice view was a very entertaining gray squirrel who scurried up and down a tree with his winter stash, much to the delight of our two-year-old daughter Katie. For a while, he sat on a branch nibbling on a berry while we watched and Katie squealed, then he was gone in search of more food. The squirrel's preparedness prompted several locals to predict an earlier than

normal winter.

I was not ready to think about snowfall yet. So after a hearty breakfast of cinnamon rolls, eggs, bacon, hashbrowns, and coffee, we headed out to hike the nature trails, and then over to the hot springs for a dip in the pool.

Later that morning, Jan took me on a brief tour of the lodge, leading me through French doors and down a short set of steps to the first of several meeting rooms. He explained that groups rent the rooms for corporate meetings, wedding receptions, or small conventions. Most of the rooms are connected and offer a luxurious way to conduct business or celebrate an important day.

One of the most elegant rooms was being converted from a billiard room into the main dining room where the evening meal will be served. The bar, with its huge stone fireplace, large windows overlooking the grounds, and mounted wildlife, will remain as it is. And the smaller but cute dining room, now used for all meals, will be open for only breakfast and lunch.

The forty-eight room resort can accommodate up to 160 people at any one time, and there are also several rustic cabins with wood heat, port-a-potties, and wash basins available for guest use. The newer hotel rooms are in an apartment-style building with eight rooms, and there are several suites available.

Our stay at Chena Hot Springs was all too short, but for our trip back down the highway, Jan had the kitchen staff pack up sandwiches, fruit, and small round bottles of apple juice.

ACCOMMODATIONS: For reservations or more information write to Chena Hot Springs, Drawer 25, 1919 Lathrop Street, Fairbanks, Alaska 99701, or telephone (907) 452-7867. The resort is open year-round. Reservations are required 2 weeks in advance. A $25, nonrefundable deposit is required for cabins only. Chena Hot Springs accepts MasterCard, American Express, Visa, cash, and personal checks. The rates are: $43 to $83 per night for small cabins, $83 to $103 per night for large cabins, and $48 to $98 per night for a hotel room. The resort also offers a 15 percent discount for groups of 15 or more, and weekend specials during the winter months. Rates include room, linens, towels, and use of the hot springs. Depending on rate, room has either a sink and toilet or a full bathroom with shower. Meals are served in the main dining room between 7:00 A.M. and 10:00 P.M. Children are welcome, but currently there are no special items for infants or young children.

TRAVEL INFORMATION: The resort is accessible by car or plane only. From Fairbanks drive the Steese Highway north 4.5 miles to the Chena Hot Springs Road, turn left and drive 56.5 miles to the resort. The road is paved, and driving is good. The drive takes approximately 1 hour. The resort also offers a 3,000-foot airstrip for private pilots or charter flights.

ARCTIC CIRCLE
HOT SPRINGS RESORT
Central

I n ancient times, mythologists tell us, it was believed that the gods called forth natural spring waters from subterranean mineral pools when they wanted to quench their thirst. By the early 1900s, gold miners were erecting tent bathhouses around, and frolicking in, the hot spring waters bubbling forth from what must have been some of those same subterranean pools.

But by the time I arrived at Circle Hot Springs, the gods and the miners had disappeared. Instead, I found a creamy yellow, three-story summer resort with decks dappled by brown- and yellow-striped umbrellas shading round wooden tables, and a hot springs full of relaxed guests.

The hot springs, discovered by gold miner William Greats in 1893, is eighty miles south of the Arctic Circle located in the old mining community of Central, Alaska. In the early 1900s, homesteaders Frank and Emma Leach put up tent bathhouses for local gold seekers. In fact, many miners wintered over at the hot springs waiting for spring breakup. Instead of chipping snow and ice from creek beds, the miners found they often had to chip ice away from the bathhouse door in order to get in. The hot, soothing water must have been worth the fight, because the gold miners returned to Central every year while gold could be found in the nearby creeks.

Many of the original small log cabins built by either the Leaches or early miners still stand as monuments to life in early Alaska. One has been converted into a bakery that serves luscious pecan rolls, another into a mercantile store with shelves stocked with everything from beautiful red fox pelts to Pampers. Some of the cabins are still available for guest use, but they are rustic.

Across Main Street stands the Arctic Circle Hot Springs Hotel, built in 1930, and its cement hot springs pool. The hotel's

manager Bob LeRude explained that since the mineral water comes out of the ground at a scalding temperature of 139 degrees (Fahrenheit), it is cooled down through a system of pipes and then pumped into the cement guest pool. It was a little past 5:00 P.M. and about 40 degrees when we decided to brave the rain and chill to take a dip in the hot springs.

The smell of sulfur was everywhere — a natural companion of mineral hot springs. We scurried from the hotel to the bathhouse already clad in our bathing suits and with towels wrapped around us for some warmth. Leaving the dry towels inside the bathhouse, we quickly jumped into the steamy water for a needed thirty minutes of relaxation before heading back in for dinner.

The hotel itself is extremely charming, done in Victorian decor, there are lace curtains and an array of tastefully arranged dried flowers on table tops and in the adjoining restaurant. The lobby offers a sitting area with television, where the air becomes heavy with cigarette smoke by late afternoon. In addition to the cozy dining room and a fairly noisy bar in the log cabin next door, the hotel offers three floors of single and double rooms, each decorated with different wallpaper accents and reproduction antiques.

Each floor has two communal bathrooms (one on each floor has a Jacuzzi bath) with sink, toilet, and shower. And for a little more money, guests can reserve a private suite with a private Jacuzzi.

ACCOMMODATIONS: For reservations or more information write to Bob and Loretta LeRude, Arctic Circle Hot Springs Resort, Central, Alaska 99730, or telephone (907) 520-5113. The resort is open year-round. Reservations are necessary. A 50 percent deposit is required to confirm a reservation. The deposit is fully refunded with cancellation 48 hours in advance of arrival date, or if weather prevents guests from reaching the hotel. Arctic Circle accepts cash and personal checks only. The rates are: $35 per night for single occupancy, $40 to $115 per night for cabins, and $85 per night for a deluxe suite with Jacuzzi. The resort also offers a fourth floor hostel at $15 a person per night. Rates include room, linens, towels, and unlimited use of the hot springs, showers, and Jacuzzis. The resort offers a main dining room. During the summer months, hours are 7:00 A.M. to 11:00 P.M. daily. During winter months breakfast is served from 7:00 A.M. to 10:00 A.M., lunch from 12:00 P.M. to 2:00 P.M., and dinner from 6:00 P.M. to 8:00 P.M. Meals range from hamburgers and chili to a hearty buffet dinner on Saturday night and a champagne brunch on Sunday morning. The area offers historic sight-seeing. Drive 32 miles north to the historic mining community of Circle and take a boat excursion up the Yukon River. The area is great for hiking and canoeing. Children are welcome. The resort has one small cradle for infants. Request for cradle should be made when reservations are made. There are no other special items for infants or young children.

TRAVEL INFORMATION: The resort is accessible by car and plane only. Most guests fly to Fairbanks and rent a car for the 134-mile drive to the resort. From Fairbanks drive north on the Steese Highway. At Fox, Alaska, bear right continuing on the Steese. The first 44 miles are paved allowing for an average speed of 55 miles per hour. The remaining 90 miles traverse some bad stretches, winding through steep mountain passes and narrow switchbacks. The road is slippery when wet, and the going can be very slow. At Central, turn east on the Hot Springs Road. The resort is 8 miles at the end of the road. The drive takes approximately 4 hours. Between June and August, KAK Tours provides scheduled round-trip, small-van service from Fairbanks to the resort at $60. Special tours can be arranged in May and September. For reservations or more information, write KAK Tours, 1215 Choctaw Road, Fairbanks, Alaska 99705, or call (907) 488-2649. There is a 4,375-foot airstrip for private pilots or charter flights.

ADDITIONAL LODGING

Trapper Creek to the Arctic Circle including
Denali National Park and Preserve

PIRATE LAKE CABINS
Pirate Lake

This is the lakeside estate of the late mountaineer Ray Genet who, with the help of friends, built each of the guest log cabins by hand. The eighty-acre estate is now maintained by his partner Kathy Sullivan. She rents the cabins during the summer months to hikers and photographers. During the winter months, outdoor guide Kevin Fitzgerald takes over the operation and offers cross-country ski outings and wintertime excursions.

Each cabin looks directly into the face of the Ruth Glacier and Mount McKinley, each is well maintained and has a wood stove. A central kitchen and dining hall complete the facilities. But for all their beauty, the cabins are rustic. There are no bathing facilities or outhouses.

Kevin says the surrounding terrain is excellent for the experienced hiker, and an abundance of wildlife puts the photography in high demand. But, he warns that bears are also abundant in the surrounding woods. So those who use the cabins should come *mentally* prepared for encounters with bears. If you should encounter a bear, slowly back away from the animal. If the bear follows, try yelling or making loud noises to frighten the animal off. It is best to check with the Alaska Department of Fish and Game for regulations regarding firearms and how to report a bear kill before embarking on a wilderness trip. See Introduction for specific tips on preparing for bear encounters.

ACCOMMODATIONS: For reservations or more information write to Kevin Fitzgerald, c/o Pirate Lake Cabins, Talkeetna, Alaska 99676, or telephone (907) 733-2704. The cabins are open year-round. Reservations are necessary 60 days in advance of winter trips. A 15 percent deposit is required to confirm the reservation. Consult owners on deposit refund. Pirate Lake accepts cash or traveler's checks only. The rate is $20 per night per cabin. Rate includes cabin only. Guests must bring own food, sleeping bag, and cooking utensils. Round-trip air transportation is available in Talkeetna at $180 per person. Rate for a winter ski package is $95 per night per person. Rate includes guided cross-country ski trips along the Ruth River or into the spectacular Ruth Amphitheater, food, and accommodations. Guests must bring own sleeping bag, ski equipment, warm clothing, and personal items. Children are welcome, but currently there are no special items for infants or young children.

TRAVEL INFORMATION: The cabins are accessible by float-plane, jet boat, dog sled, or cross-country skis. In summer months, Fitzgerald says, guests may want to jet boat up the river for a few days of hiking or photography and then raft back to Talkeetna. Fitzgerald or Sullivan will make all travel arrangements from Talkeetna. Also there are several air taxi operators in Talkeetna that will fly guests into the cabins.

DENALI WILDERNESS LODGE
AT WOOD RIVER
Denali National Park and Preserve

L ynn and Penny Castle say that stepping off the airplane at Wood River is like stepping back into the early 1900s. "Things have changed little since the gold rush and fur trader days when the original cabins were built," they said.

The lodge is located east of Denali National Park and Preserve in the remote Wood River valley of the Central Alaska Range. Guests stay in the hand-hewn log guest house with its own living room and open stove with fireplace. The six individual rooms have both single and double beds. Full bathing facilities also are offered. In addition to the guest house, the Castles offer several rustic log cabins for family groups or for the more adventurous.

ACCOMMODATIONS: For reservations or more information write to Lynn and Penny Castle, Denali Wilderness Lodge at Wood River, P.O. Box 517, Denali National Park and Preserve, Alaska 99755, or telephone Denali Wilderness Air at (907) 683-2261. The lodge is open 15 May through 25 September. Reservations are required at least 6 months in advance. But space available reservations are accepted during the summer season. A 25 percent deposit is required to confirm reservation. Consult owners on deposit refund. Denali Wilderness Lodge accepts MasterCard, Visa, American Express, cash, and personal checks. The rates are: $225 per night per person or $750 per person for a maximum stay of 5 nights. Rates include round-trip transportation from the park (add $150 if travel originates in Fairbanks), all meals, and guided hikes or horseback trail trips. Children are welcome, but currently there are no special items for infants or young children.

TRAVEL INFORMATION: The lodge is accessible by plane only.

Cost is included in lodge rate. Independent travelers can make arrangements through Denali Wilderness Air, located at the railroad station in Denali National Park and Preserve, telephone (907) 683-2261. To reach the park by car from Anchorage, drive the George Parks Highway north 237 miles to the park entrance. The drive takes approximately 5 hours. From Fairbanks drive the George Parks Highway south 120 miles to the park entrance. The drive takes approximately 2.5 hours. Transportation to the park also is available via the Alaska Railroad. For reservations and more information contact the railroad at (907) 265-2494. In Seattle, Washington, the number is (206) 624-4234. Train reservations should be made 2 weeks prior to travel.

McKINLEY WILDERNESS LODGE
Denali National Park and Preserve

Sitting along the banks of Carlo Creek, about six miles south of the entrance to Denali National Park and Preserve, are fifteen sleeping cabins owned and operated by Karen and Ron Bitzer. The duplex-style cabins, each with a double bed, writing table with chairs, propane heat, and electric lights, are a nice stop-off for a night while visiting the park. There are several cute A-frame cabins on the south bank of Carlo Creek. A bridge over the creek joins the entire camp.

McKinley Wilderness Lodge also offers a clean central bathhouse with shower, toilets, and sinks. Linens are provided, and even at the height of the tourist season, there never seems to be a line. There are also several picnic sites sprinkled throughout the camp.

ACCOMMODATIONS: For reservations or more information write to Karen and Ron Bitzer, McKinley Wilderness Lodge, P.O. Box 85, Denali National Park and Preserve, Alaska 99755, or telephone (907) 683-2277. The cabins are open 31 May through 1 September. Reservations are required 3 weeks in advance. A $65 deposit confirms the reservation. Deposits are fully refunded with cancellation 7 days in advance of arrival date, or if cabin can be resold to another party. McKinley Wilderness Lodge accepts Visa, MasterCard, and personal checks. The rate is $65 per night per cabin. Each cabin sleeps up to 4 people. Rate includes cabin, linens, towels, propane heat, and round-trip transportation from the railroad station in the park. Meals are not served, but several nice restaurants are located just minutes away, and barbecue grills are located on the grounds. Children are welcome, and the lodge provides baby cribs upon request.

TRAVEL INFORMATION: The lodge is accessible by car, train,

or plane. From Anchorage drive north on the George Parks Highway to Milepost 224. The drive takes approximately 5 hours. From Fairbanks drive south on the George Parks Highway 120 miles to the lodge. The drive takes approximately 2.5 hours. Transportation also is available via the Alaska Railroad. For reservations or more information contact the railroad at (907) 265-2494. In Seattle, Washington, the number is (206) 624-4234. Train reservations should be made 2 weeks prior to travel. An airstrip is located within the park for private pilots or charter flights. Guests traveling by train or plane should notify the lodge so that courtesy transportation to the guest cabins can be arranged.

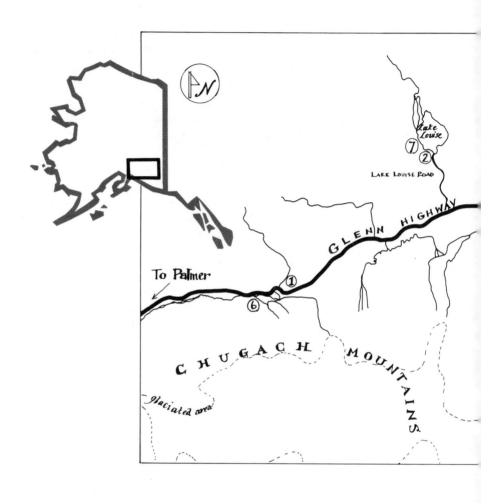

EASTERN HIDEAWAYS
Palmer to McCarthy

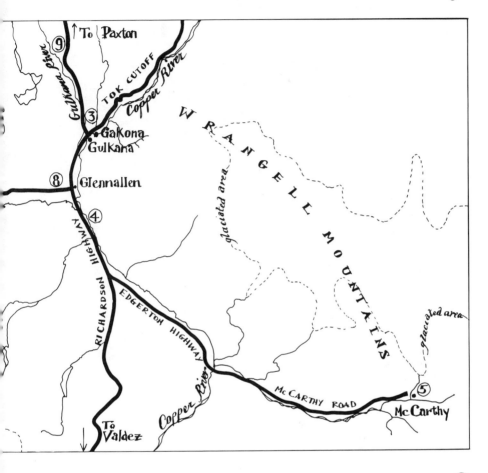

SHEEP MOUNTAIN LODGE
Sheep Mountain

The setting at Sheep Mountain Lodge could be a rough cut of an artist's block print—the fireweed, lupine, and wild orchids; the mountains and rivers; the small rustic cabins. It is a good place to cross-country ski during the winter months. It is the perfect place to stop for lodging on the way into or out of the city.

Owners Debi and Sherman Reams bought the lodge in 1981 and have worked hard to build up its reputation and clientele. Now they find the cabins booked most weekends when the snow is best—mid-February through mid-April—and during the summer months when driving the Glenn Highway is easiest.

Skiers come to tackle ski runs with names like Corkscrew and Thrill Run and to soak in the sauna afterward. Some people even make the drive just to carry home a jug of Sheep Mountain's artesian water. Sherman made some major improvements to some of the trails when they first took over the management. Since then he has added more trails to make a fifteen-kilometer ski circuit.

"It probably looks the same to a lot of people who don't realize the amount of work that has gone into improving the lodge," he said. "But it really is different."

ACCOMMODATIONS: For reservations or more information write to Debi and Sherman Reams, Sheep Mountain Lodge, SRC 8490, Palmer, Alaska 99645, or telephone (907) 745-5121. The lodge is open year-round. Reservations are required at least 2 weeks in advance. A $45 deposit is required. Deposit is fully refunded with cancellation 24 hours before arrival. Sheep Mountain Lodge accepts cash and personal checks only. The rate is $45 per night for double occupancy and $5 for each additional person. Rate includes cabin

and linens. A private bath is available during the summer months only. A central bath is available year-round. Meals are available in the main lodge. There is a cross-country ski-trail system nearby. Children are welcome, but currently there are no special items for infants or young children.

TRAVEL INFORMATION: The lodge is accessible by car only. From Anchorage or Palmer drive the Glenn Highway to Mile-post 113. The drive is beautiful, as the highway winds through the Chugach Mountains toward the Wrangell Mountains. Sheep Mountain Lodge is set back only a short distance from the highway on the left-hand side of the road as you drive away from Palmer.

THE EVERGREEN LODGE
Lake Louise

The Evergreen Lodge sits at the end of a long, country road on the banks of sparkling Lake Louise. But do not let its backcountry setting give the impression this is a sleepy place. This rustic lodge bustles with activity generated by lodge owners Paul and Cheryl Holland, by the locals who wander in for a mid-afternoon beer or cup of coffee, and by the guests themselves who come here to ski, fish, and enjoy lakeside relaxation.

"I guess if I had to choose one word to describe it, I'd say 'comfortable.' It is a comfortable place, and the people who come here are pampered," Paul told me.

We had planned on a dinnertime arrival at Evergreen, but we got there about two hours early. I could smell something wonderful cooking. Paul said the evening's bill of fare included prime rib with Yorkshire pudding, and he said it so nonchalantly that I thought such gourmet meals must be a commonplace at Evergreen. Indeed, the weekend menus do not change, Paul said. There is prime rib on Saturday night and a champagne brunch on Sunday mornings. Pampered, I thought, is putting it mildly.

It has taken awhile for the Hollands to transform their home into a sophisticated lodge. They bought Evergreen in 1978, and although they both have been in the innkeeping business most of their lives, Paul said Evergreen presented challenges.

At a rustic wilderness lodge, he added, "You just have to be a jack-of-all-trades. You have to be an airplane, boat, and auto mechanic, be able to fix refrigerators, build cabins, guide skiers, entertain guests, and make a great martini." Cheryl has always insisted on "doing things up right," Paul said. And their perseverance has paid off.

The weekend we were there, Cheryl was in the hospital about to give birth to their third child, and Paul seemed to have his hands full. So we left to allow him to tend to the rigors of readying dinner for twenty people. After settling into our little log cottage, we took a walking tour of the area.

We discovered that each of the six guest cabins sleep four people and has propane heat, warm blankets, and electric light. All the cabins sit off to the right of the main lodge, each in its own thicket of trees, but with views of the lake. The central bath and shower is in the main lodge as is the dining room. The main lodge was built of hand-peeled logs in 1948. Since that time, the lodge has been enlarged, and the interior has been paneled with sheets of knotty pine, but the large hand-peeled ridge beams running the length of the dining room and main lounge stand as a reminder of the early craftsmanship.

By the time we heard the clanging of the brass dinner bell, the sun was beginning to set over Lake Louise. The pink and golden sky slowly fell victim to the encroaching night. But inside the lodge, as we made our way through the buffet line, we hardly noticed. All the meals at Evergreen are served family style in the dining area, a knotty pine paneled room with several long tables. Paul played chef, carving huge slabs of prime rib and lifting them gently onto begging plates. To accompany the meat, the Evergreen cooks had prepared Yorkshire pudding, baked potatoes, English peas and homemade banana bread. And for dessert: homemade blueberry ice cream with huge, handpicked berries, heaped over rich pound cake. Pampered was putting it mildly.

ACCOMMODATIONS: For reservations or more information write to Paul and Cheryl Holland, The Evergreen Lodge at Lake Louise, SRC Box 8867, Lake Louise, Alaska 99645, or telephone (907) 822-3250. The lodge is open year-round. Reservations are required. A 50 percent deposit is required. The deposit is fully refunded with cancellation 14 days before arrival. There are 5 log guest cabins and 1 frame guest cabin. The rates are: $45 per night, per person, Sunday through Thursday, includes dinner and breakfast; $55 for Friday night, includes dinner and breakfast; and $75 for Saturday night, includes the prime rib dinner and Sunday champagne brunch. The weekend package is $110 per person and includes lodging for 3 days and 2 nights, all meals, and use of the sauna. Boat rental is $10 per hour plus gas, and canoe rental is $5 per hour. Children are welcome, and Evergreen offers children an assortment of toys in the lodge, high chairs, small drinking glasses, and toddler-size plates. There are no cribs or playpens.

TRAVEL INFORMATION: The lodge is accessible by car only. From Anchorage or Palmer drive the Glenn Highway north to Milepost 159.8. Turn left at the sign for Lake Louise and drive 15 miles until you see the signs for the Evergreen. From Glennallen or Valdez, the Lake Louise turnoff is at Milepost 168.2.

GAKONA LODGE & TRADING POST
Gakona

Dusk was beginning to gather around the Gakona Lodge and settle over Mount Sanford looming on the not-too-distant horizon. The car's headlights cast a long shadow of the hitching post over the pebble-strewn grass as we pulled up. The trees rustled in the wind almost as if to announce our presence. It was the perfect time to arrive at Gakona.

We entered the Carriage House Restaurant through heavy wooden barn doors, stepping into a small foyer and then down a few steps into the larger dining room where candles flickered in small red jars atop red linen tablecloths. The room is named after its original function. It was, in fact, the carriage house where patrons of the early roadhouse, known as Doyle's Ranch, boarded their steeds for the night.

I had heard about Gakona Lodge a few years ago from a friend of mine who rafted the nearby Gulkana River and spent a couple of nights patronizing the lodge and Trapper's Den bar. "It is one of the most rustic and atmospheric places I've ever stayed at in Alaska," he said.

In its heyday, the lodge also must have been one of the most elaborate stops along the heavily traveled road from Valdez to Fairbanks and Eagle. The original lodge was built in 1905, made of saddle-corner log construction with a floor of whipsawn lumber. After the road was improved for stagecoach travel in 1910, Gakona became a stop for the Orr Stage Co. A barn suitable for twelve horses and a blacksmith's shop were built. And then in 1929, the larger lodge — the one used today — was built. Some of the original log structures put up in 1902 still stand along the banks of the Gakona River behind the current lodge.

When Barbara, Jerry, and John Strang bought the road-house ten years ago, they restored the old log carriage house and converted it into a restaurant. Now patrons leave their iron steeds out front and mosey in for a wonderful evening in the large, dimly lit, log dining room with its open trusses and California wine list.

We took a table next to the window overlooking the Gakona River. A big, potbellied Yukon stove occupied one corner casting warmth across the log room filled with ancient mining and trapping relics and mounted wildlife. Between waiting tables and preparing pastries and desserts for the coming week, Barbara took time to chat with us.

All three Strangs moved to Alaska from upstate New York when Jerry and John decided the lodge appealed to their love of the wilderness. All three have specific tasks to keep the lodge running. And even as we spoke, Jerry was out back roasting our steaks on their half-barrel charcoal barbecue, and John was next door at the Trapper's Den bar drawing our frosty draft beer from the tap.

Given the time, Jerry and John will talk your ear off, filling you in on local history and bringing those interested up to date on the antics of the ghost that supposedly inhabits guest room No. 5. The ghost, it is said, likes to blow smoke in people's faces, control the loudness of music, romp up and down the stairs, and converse with

whomever in the middle of the night. A harmless, but pesky ghost it seems.

It was nearly 10:00 P.M. before we readied ourselves to leave the Carriage House. The moon was full and although it was only August, the Wrangell Mountains were covered with a healthy dose of early snow — or termination dust as Alaskans call it. The Trapper's Den was quiet, and the lodge was darkened, but everywhere we looked we saw evidence of the warmth and hospitality that surely has inhabited Gakona Lodge since the first carriage pulled up and the driver tethered its reins to the hitching post.

ACCOMMODATIONS: For reservations or more information write to the Strangs, Gakona Lodge & Trading Post, Box 285, Gakona, Alaska 99586, or telephone (907) 822-3482. The lodge, on the National Register of Historic Places, is open from mid-March to 1 January. Reservations are required. A deposit is not required. The lodge has 10 guest rooms. The rates are: $25 per night single occupancy, $45 double occupancy, and $15 for each additional person. Children are welcome, but currently there are no special items for infants or young children.

TRAVEL INFORMATION: The lodge is accessible by car or plane only. Two main overland routes cross at Glennallen, Alaska — the Richardson and the Glenn highways. At that junction, take the Tok cutoff and drive east 15 miles. The lodge is on the left-hand side of the road. Private pilots or charter flights will find an airstrip in Glennallen. Call the FAA for more information.

COPPER CENTER LODGE &
TRADING POST
Copper Center

In 1897 the Copper Center Lodge was actually a tent in which its owners dished up warm meals and provided gold seekers with a night's lodging. It was the first roadhouse in the Copper River valley, and when the gold rush trail of 1898 shifted south to Copper Center, so did the lodge. The original tent was discarded in favor of a log roadhouse, and the name changed several times, from the Hohman Hotel to Blix's Roadhouse. But today, despite those transitions, one element remains constant: owner Katherine Ashby still provides travelers a warm bed, great meals, and some of the best homemade pie around.

Since purchasing it in 1948, Katherine said the roadhouse has survived several additional major events — the 1964 earthquake that devastated Valdez and Cordova, the construction of the trans-Alaska pipeline from the North Slope of Alaska right past the roadhouse to the terminal in Valdez, and the trend toward modernizing the historic.

"We had to renovate the roadhouse to update it to modern standards," Katherine said. "We put bathrooms in each room. The lobby used to have a big Yukon stove, and we took that out. We got rid of the old iron beds with the springs that squeaked."

Today, the Copper Center Lodge is a homey place. The lobby invites guests to settle in with the morning newspaper, or relax in the adjoining restaurant with a fresh cup of coffee and some of the famous Copper Center Lodge apple pie. The guest rooms are in the best tradition of early roadhouses, clean, comfortable but very Spartan. The type of room you would expect a gold miner to fall into after a hard day on the creeks.

ACCOMMODATIONS: For reservations or more information write

to Katherine Ashby, Copper Center Lodge & Trading Post, Box 805, Copper Center, Alaska 99573, or telephone (907) 822-3245. The roadhouse is open year-round. Reservations are necessary 2 weeks in advance. A deposit is not required. Copper Center Lodge accepts MasterCard, Visa, cash, and traveler's checks. There are 20 guest rooms at the lodge. The rates are: $40 per night for single occupancy, $45 for double occupancy with private bath, and $80 for two rooms with a shared bath. Rates include room, linens, and towels. Meals are served in the dining room. Children are welcome, but currently there are no special items for infants or young children.

TRAVEL INFORMATION: The lodge is accessible by car only. From Glennallen drive 15 miles south on the Richardson Highway. Watch for "Historic Site" signs, which will direct you to Copper Center and the roadhouse. From Valdez drive the Richardson Highway north 101 miles to the roadhouse. From Anchorage drive the Glenn Highway 189 miles north to Glennallen, then the Richardson Highway to the roadhouse for a total distance of 203 miles.

THE McCARTHY LODGE
McCarthy

There are many memorable aspects of McCarthy and its rustic inn. But surely one of the most memorable experiences is getting there. The road to McCarthy starts out tame enough. Nineteen miles of paved highway, after you first leave the Richardson Highway, takes you past agricultural homesteads, then the pavement ends and a good gravel road pushes you up into the Wrangell Mountains with breathtaking views of the beautiful Copper River below. At Milepost 23.6, most travelers turn into Liberty Falls campground where thundering Liberty Falls makes a great backdrop for photographs. Just before you arrive at Chitina (pronounced CHIT' na) — established in 1908 as a rail stop along the Copper River and Northwestern Railway to serve the Kennecott Copper Mines — the road becomes a little narrower.

Outside of town, across the Copper River valley, the road closes in on cars, leaving little room for passing. The road's shoulder seems to have little substance, and we found the turnouts overlooking the Copper River to be the only safe way to pull over. As you begin a slow climb into the mountains, the road becomes nothing more than gravel laid on top of the abandoned wooden rail ties. The jolting ride will continue as the car encounters other potholes and large rocks to hobble over. Conversation is reduced to a minimum.

Then you come upon The Bridge, a single-lane railroad truss approximately 283 feet above the rushing torrents of the Kuskulana River. You know there is a river down there, because you can see it through the planks and over the edge of the two-foot-high guard rail.

The road stops about a mile outside of McCarthy at the Kennicott River. From there, the only way across the river and into town is via the two-seater, hand-pulled tram. Be prepared for a short hike, another tram ride, and another short walk before getting to McCarthy.

And then there it is, McCarthy, tucked into the midst of the Wrangell-St. Elias National Park and Preserve. Some think they have

just reached Eden. Calving glaciers, rugged mountains, a rustic little mining community is how a lot of people envision most of Alaska.

For nearly thirty years, McCarthy was the economic center for copper mining at the Kennecott mines six miles outside of town. Between 1910 and 1938, millions of dollars in copper ore were taken out of the mines there. Miners who could not get housing for their families at the mine site, lodged them in McCarthy, and the McCarthy Lodge gave the miners a place to spend their money on liquor and gambling.

But that was fifty years ago. The abandoned Kennecott Copper Mine is now a national historic landmark, and the McCarthy Lodge caters to those who want to forgo luxury for rustic wilderness, and wander, if even for a short time, through the area's past. The lodge is a relic and is full of relics. Moose antlers hang from above the windows on the outside of the lodge. Glacial ice taken from the nearby Kennicott Glacier cools the old wooden ice house. The rooms are plain — a bed, a bare light bulb — the meals are hearty, and visitors are more than welcome.

ACCOMMODATIONS: For reservations or more information write to the McCarthy Lodge, McCarthy, Alaska 99588. The lodge does not have a phone, but those wanting to make reservations by phone should call (907) 562-2161 and leave a message. The manager will return the call. The lodge, on the National Register of Historic Places, is open from May through September. Reservations are preferred. A deposit is not required. The McCarthy Lodge accepts cash and traveler's checks only. There is a fourplex next to the lodge and a bunkhouse across the street. The rates are: $95 per night for single occupancy, meals and shower included; $135 per night for double occupancy, meals not included; and $15 per night for a bunkhouse bed. Showers are $5 per person. Meals are served family style in the lodge's dining room. The menu is generally limited. The lodge also rents Schwinn bikes at $10 a day, $6 a half-day. Children are welcome, but currently there are no special items for infants or young children.

TRAVEL INFORMATION: The lodge is accessible by car or plane only. From the Richardson Highway turn onto the Edgerton Highway and follow it 96 miles to McCarthy. The drive is slow, approximately 3 to 5 hours, due to poor road conditions. McCarthy also has an airstrip for private pilots or charter flights. Charters out of Glennallen are available and cost about $540 round trip. Also, on Tuesdays, a mail plane runs mail and supplies into McCarthy. If seats are available, the cost is $60 per trip.

ADDITIONAL LODGING

Palmer to McCarthy

LONG RIFLE LODGE
Glacier View

There once was a small, two-year-old black bear who, unfortunately, played on the highway in front of the Long Rifle Lodge. Now he stands, mounted in the dining room of the lodge along with myriad other wildlife. Lynne and Eugene Whitmill believe in making their lodge and restaurant as Alaskan as possible. And they have succeeded.

The large picture windows of the cozy dining room offer a spectacular view of the Matanuska Glacier and the Chugach Mountains, and Lynne has left a pair of binoculars on the windowsill for those who want a closer look. While we waited for our hamburgers and chili, I perused the Chugach Mountains through binoculars looking for Dall sheep, bear, and other animals. Other guests took turns at the coin-operated telescope on the nearby veranda.

The balcony embraces the three nicest guest rooms, which are part of the main lodge. These rooms have the same view of the glacier and mountains as does the restaurant. They include private baths with shower, double or queen-size bed, and at least one twin bed. But Long Rifle also offers eight other rooms in a prefabricated motel-style unit next to the main lodge. Some of them have full baths, some only half-baths.

After a tour of the rooms and a leisurely stroll along the deck amid the hanging flowers and potted plants, I went back to enjoy my lunch.

ACCOMMODATIONS: For reservations or more information write to Lynne and Eugene Whitmill, Long Rifle Lodge, SRC Box 8445, Palmer, Alaska 99645, or telephone (907) 745-5151. The lodge is open year-round. Reservations should be made 1 week prior to arrival. A $10 deposit is required. Consult owners on deposit refund.

Long Rifle Lodge accepts MasterCard, Visa, cash, and personal checks. The rates are: $35 per night for rooms with half-baths, $45 per night for rooms with full baths, and $10 for each additional person. Rates include room, linens, and towels. Meals are served in the main lodge. Children are welcome, but currently there are no special items for infants or young children.

TRAVEL INFORMATION: The lodge is accessible by car only. From Anchorage or Palmer drive the Glenn Highway north 102 miles. The lodge is on the right-hand side of the road. From Glennallen the lodge is 138 miles.

WOLVERINE LODGE
Lake Louise

T he original Wolverine Lodge burned down several years ago, and as a result the lodge has a modern, new look to it. Cathedral ceilings with tongue-and-groove decking, a huge rock fireplace in the main sitting area, and a cocktail lounge separated from the main room by the fireplace are all hallmarks of the new Wolverine.

Owner Peggy Dicks helps prepare all meals and keeps her kitchen open 16 hours out of every day so that if a hungry sailor comes in off the water, a bill of fare will be available anytime.

"I figure people come up here to get away from being on a schedule, not to have to watch the clock," Peggy said. Perhaps because of the open kitchen, Wolverine Lodge is a favorite stopping off point for a sandwich or a beer, and the cocktail lounge has become a favorite gathering spot for locals during the evening hours.

ACCOMMODATIONS: For reservations or more information write to Allen and Peggy Dicks, Wolverine Lodge, Lake Louise, Alaska 99646. Wolverine Lodge has no telephone. Guests must call radio station KCAM at (907) 822-3022 and leave a message with the Caribou Clatter program. Allen or Peggy will call you back. The lodge is open year-round. Reservations are preferred. A deposit is not necessary. The lodge has 10 modern rooms in the main lodge, all have private sinks and toilets. A common shower is available at the end of the hall. The rate is $35 per night per person and $5 for each additional person. All linens are furnished. Children are welcome, but currently there are no special items for infants or young children.

TRAVEL INFORMATION: The lodge is accessible by car only. From Anchorage or Palmer drive the Glenn Highway north to Milepost 159.8. Turn left at the sign for Lake Louise and drive

15 miles until you see the signs for the Wolverine. From Glennallen or Valdez take the Lake Louise turnoff at Milepost 168.2.

Twin Flower

TOLSONA LAKE RESORT
Tolsona Lake

T he resort is one-quarter of a mile off the Glenn Highway and is quiet, clean, and run by two very nice people, Julie and Kirk Wilson. Food here is always ample—a thick prime rib dinner on Saturday night, an all-you-can-eat sourdough pancake breakfast on Sunday morning. The main lodge offers a huge cocktail lounge and restaurant for dining and after-dinner recreation. Guests can choose between several rustic cabins or five modern motel rooms along the shore of Tolsona Lake.

ACCOMMODATIONS: For reservations or more information write to Julie and Kirk Wilson, Tolsona Lake Resort, SRC Box 8900, Palmer, Alaska 99645, or telephone (907) 822-3433. The resort is open year-round. Reservations are not necessary during summer months. During winter months, the Wilsons need a 2-day notice in order to heat up cabins. Summer rates are: $34 per night for single occupancy and $40 for double occupancy. Winter rates are: $30 per night for single occupancy, and $35 for double occupancy. Each additional person is $8. The Wilsons also offer a 2-day special during winter months. Rate for 4 or fewer guests is $32 per night per person including breakfast and dinner. Rate for 5 to 8 guests is $30 per night per person. Rate for more than 8 guests is $28 per day per person.

TRAVEL INFORMATION: The lodge is accessible by car or plane only. From Anchorage drive north on the Glenn Highway to Milepost 170. Turn left at sign for Tolsona Lake and drive ¼ mile to the resort. A 2,000-foot runway is available for private pilots or charter flights. Tolsona Lake is available for floatplanes.

SOURDOUGH ROADHOUSE
Sourdough Creek

The roadhouse, said to be the oldest of all gold stampede roadhouses in the state, was built in 1903 when gold miners regularly traveled the Fairbanks-to-Valdez route. The Sourdough is listed on the National Register of Historic Places and still operates from the original log building.

Although roadhouses traditionally have been places where travelers spend one night while on their way to somewhere else, owners Tom and Peggy Keesucker want to lure people into spending a few days at the Sourdough to learn more about local history and to make their roadhouse a place travelers will go out of their way to visit.

One reason for going out of one's way might be the Alaska-Sourdough Rocks & Relics swap shop next door to the lodge. The swap shop is owned by Bud Lauesen, former owner of the road-house, and is filled with Alaskan antiques and relics, all for sale. Browsing or buying is great fun!

ACCOMMODATIONS: For reservations or more information write to Tom and Peggy Keesucker, Sourdough Roadhouse, Sourdough Creek, Alaska 99646. The roadhouse has no phone, callers must contact radio station KCAM at (907) 822-3022 and leave a message with the Caribou Clatter program. Reservations are not necessary. A deposit is not required. Rates range from $34 to $50 per night, per person, beds in the bunkhouse cabin are $10 per night. Rates include room, linens, and towels. Rooms are simple, clean, and very Spartan. The dining room is open daily from 6:00 A.M. to 10:00 P.M. and specializes in the famous Sourdough breakfast — two eggs, ham, bacon or sausage plus all the sourdough pancakes you can eat for $5. Dinner is hamburgers, chili, sandwiches, and a house special.

Children are welcome, but currently there are no special items for infants or young children.

TRAVEL INFORMATION: The roadhouse is accessible by car. From Valdez drive the Richardson Highway north 147.5 miles to the roadhouse. From Fairbanks drive the Richardson Highway south 216.5 miles.

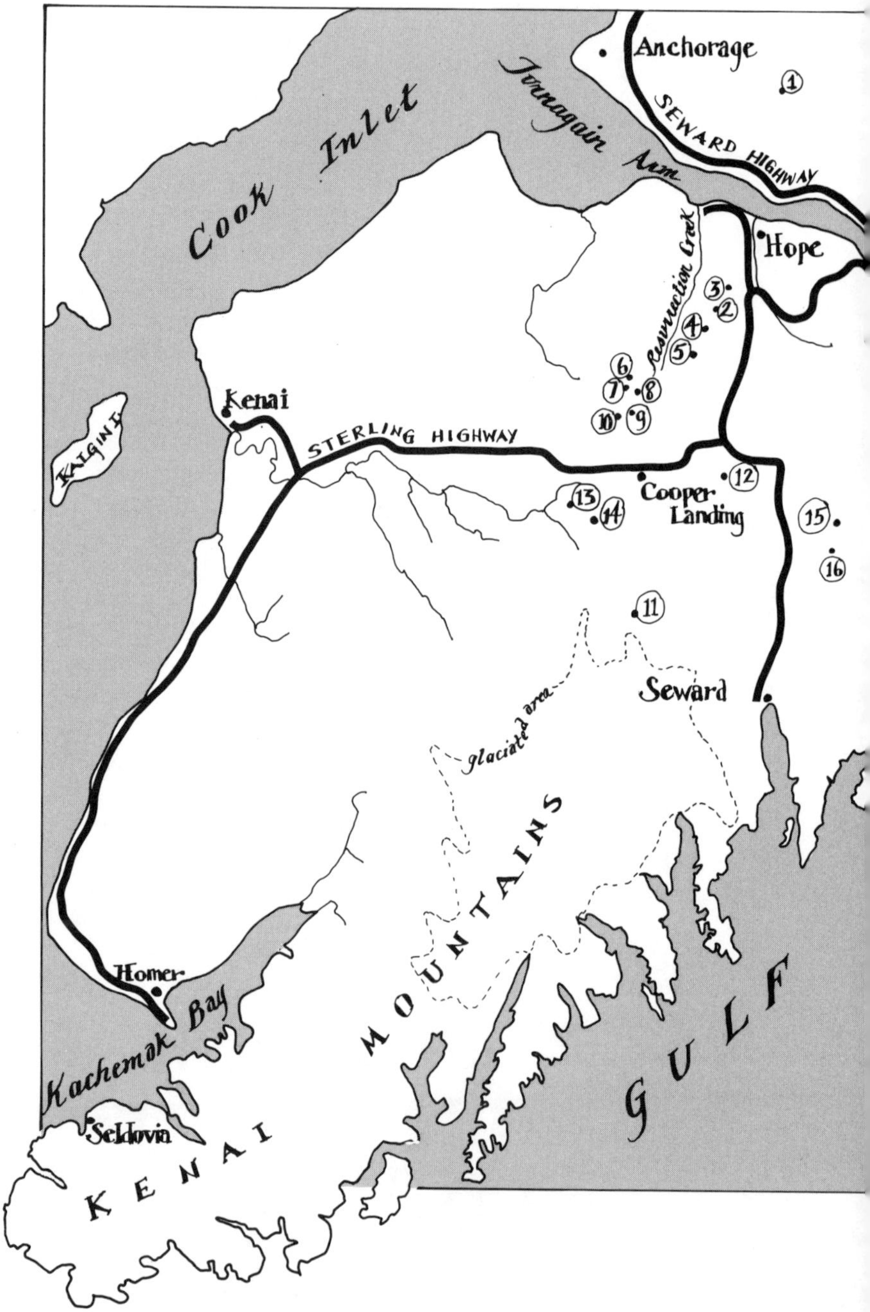

Anchorage
SEWARD HIGHWAY
Cook Inlet
Turnagain Arm
Hope
Resurrection Creek
Kenai
KALGIN I.
STERLING HIGHWAY
Cooper Landing
Seward
glaciated area
KENAI MOUNTAINS
Homer
Kachemak Bay
Seldovia
GULF
1
2
3
4
5
6
7
8
9
10
11
12
13
14
15
16

U.S. FOREST SERVICE CABINS
Chugach National Forest

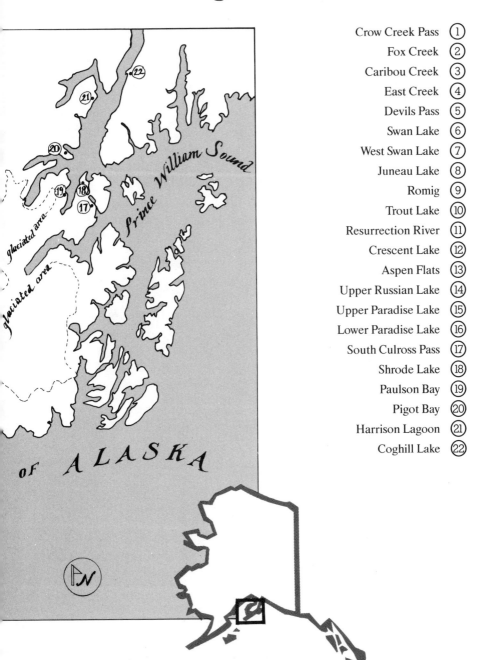

By 10:00 P.M. the daylight streaming through the cabin window was beginning to fade into twilight, but we lobbied for just a little more time to enjoy the day by lighting the small table lantern. A light but steady rain had begun to fall on the little forest service cabin at Harrison Lagoon. When our good friends Steve Lindbeck and Ginna Brelsford invited Craig and I along with another friend Michael Carey to sail to the Harrison Lagoon cabin some thirty-five miles out of Whittier, aboard their twenty-five-foot Tanzier Sloop, we readily accepted. The forest service maintains thirty-five log, Pan Abode, or A-frame cabins throughout the Chugach National Forest, from Kenai to Cordova, and we have hiked into several of them. But we had never visited the more remote cabins, accessible by only boat or floatplane.

The day the five of us set sail from the seaside village of Whittier in Prince William Sound, there was plenty of sunshine and gentle breezes. The five-hour sail was topped off by good company, beautiful scenery, and a little fishing along the way.

Our cabin was like many others the forest service maintains. Depending on the location, cabins can be rented for three days to a week. But each, no matter where it is located, offers built-in pine bunks without mattresses for four or more guests, oil or wood stoves, firewood, a rustic dining table, a kitchen cooking area, an outhouse, and a guest sign-in book.

The people who had stayed in the cabin before us had been from Michigan and Wisconsin, the folks before them from Washington State. The Great Lakes visitors had logged the most memorable events of their stay — fishing the Kenai River, kayaking, and hiking the Resurrection Trail. "Alaska must be one of the best vacation spots in the world," they wrote.

And we all agreed. Despite the evening rain, we all had enjoyed a wonderful day and a supper of freshly caught salmon. Now it was time to snuggle into the sleeping bags. Steve agreed to read aloud a short story by Mark Helprin entitled "A Vermont Tale."

As we listened to Helprin's wonderful prose, trying not to drift off to sleep, only an occasional buzz of a mosquito brought back to mind that we were miles and miles into the Alaska wilderness.

HOW TO RENT CABINS: For reservations or more information about the cabins, write the USDA Forest Service, Chugach National Forest, Attention: Cabin Reservations, 201 East 9th Avenue, Anchorage, Alaska 99501, or telephone (907) 261-2599. The rate for all cabins is $10 per night. Full payment must be made at the time reservations are requested. Payment is fully refunded if cabin is unavailable or if cancellation is made at least 10 days prior to reservation. The forest service accepts money orders or traveler's checks only if payment is mailed. Cash is accepted if payment is made in person. The forest service restricts the length of stay to a maximum of three days per group. Groups are limited to a maximum of six people per cabin. Check with the forest service regarding regulations governing the size of parties for the cabin you select. Guests must obtain a permit for cabin use by writing to the above address. Send permit application with full payment to the forest service with choice of cabin and reservation dates. Permits and confirmed reservations are issued on a first-come first-serve basis. Permits are issued if the cabin of your choice is available on the date requested. The forest service asks that all users haul out their own trash and empty cans, and that wood used for fires be replaced.

For information regarding Alaska hunting and fishing regulations, seasons, or cost of licenses write to the Alaska Department of Fish and Game, Game Division, 333 Raspberry Road, Anchorage, Alaska 99518-1599, or telephone (907) 344-0541. Specify whether hunting or fishing information is needed, or both.

KENAI PENINSULA

CROW CREEK PASS: The 16-foot square cabin is located in the Chugach Mountains, elevation 3,500 feet, and is accessible via the Crow Creek Trail 5 miles from the trailhead at the parking lot. The trail climbs steeply for 3.5 miles to the ruins of an old mining operation, then another 1.5 miles to the cabin near Raven Glacier. The cabin sleeps 10 and has a wood stove. However, the cabin is above timberline, and there is no firewood. Wildlife includes goat, sheep, moose, and black and brown bear.

FOX CREEK: The 12- by 14-foot cabin is located along the Resurrection Pass Trail, elevation 1,500 feet, and is accessible via the trail approximately 12.5 miles from the trailhead at Hope. The cabin sleeps 6 and has a wood stove. Wildlife includes moose, bear, and goat.

CARIBOU CREEK: The 12- by 14-foot cabin is located in the Kenai Mountains, elevation 1,000 feet, and is accessible via the Resurrection Pass Trail 7.1 miles from the north trailhead. The cabin sleeps 6 and has a wood stove. Wildlife includes goat, sheep, moose, and black and brown bear.

EAST CREEK: The 12- by 14-foot cabin is located in the Kenai Mountains, elevation 2,200 feet, and is accessible via the Resurrection Pass Trail 14.4 miles from the north trailhead. The cabin sleeps 6 and has a wood stove. Wildlife includes goat, sheep, moose, and black and brown bear.

DEVILS PASS: The 16-foot square cabin is located in the Kenai Mountains, elevation 2,400 feet, and is accessible via the Resurrection Pass Trail 17.1 miles from the south trailhead or over Devils Pass 10 miles from the Devils Pass trailhead. The cabin sleeps 10 and has a wood stove. However, the cabin is above timberline, and there is no firewood. Wildlife includes goat, sheep, moose, and black and brown bear.

S WAN LAKE: The 12- by 14-foot cabin is located in the Kenai Mountains, elevation 1,400 feet, and is accessible via the Resurrection Pass Trail 13 miles from the south trailhead, or by floatplane 20 minutes from Moose Pass or 15 minutes from Cooper Landing. The cabin sleeps 6 and has a wood stove. Wildlife includes caribou, moose, and black and brown bear. Lake species include lake and rainbow trout and freshwater salmon. There is a boat for fishing.

W EST SWAN LAKE: The 12- by 14-foot cabin is located in the Kenai Mountains, elevation 1,400 feet, and is accessible by floatplane only, 15 minutes from Cooper Landing. The cabin sleeps 6 and offers a wood stove. Wildlife includes caribou, moose, and black and brown bear. Lake species include lake and rainbow trout and freshwater salmon. There is a boat for fishing.

J UNEAU LAKE: The 12- by 14-foot cabin is located in the Kenai Mountains, elevation 1,300 feet, and is accessible via the Resurrection Pass Trail 10 miles from the south trailhead, or by floatplane 20 minutes from Moose Pass or 15 minutes from Cooper Landing. The cabin sleeps 6 and has a wood stove. Wildlife includes sheep, moose, and bear. Lake species include trout. There is a boat for fishing.

R OMIG: The 12- by 14-foot cabin is located in the Kenai Mountains at the south end of Juneau Lake, elevation 1,300 feet, and is accessible via the Resurrection Pass Trail 9 miles from the south trailhead or by floatplane 10 minutes from Cooper Landing. The cabin sleeps 6 and has a wood stove. Wildlife includes sheep, moose, and bear. Lake species include trout. There is a boat for fishing.

T ROUT LAKE: The 16-foot square cabin is located in the Kenai Mountains, elevation 1,300 feet, and is accessible via the Resurrection Pass Trail 7 miles from the south trailhead or by floatplane 10 minutes from Cooper Landing. The cabin sleeps 6 and has a wood stove. Wildlife includes sheep, moose, and bear. Lake species include trout. There is a boat for fishing.

RESURRECTION RIVER: The 12- by 14-foot cabin is located 1.5 miles south of Boulder Creek, elevation 600 feet, and is accessible via the Resurrection River Trail 6.5 miles from the south trailhead. The cabin sleeps 6 and has a wood stove. Wildlife includes moose and bear.

CRESCENT LAKE: The 12- by 14-foot cabin is located in the Kenai Mountains, elevation 1,454 feet, and is accessible via the Crescent Creek Trail 6.2 miles from parking area or by floatplane 15 minutes from Moose Pass or 20 minutes from Cooper Landing. The cabin sleeps 6 and has a wood stove. Wildlife includes sheep, moose, and brown and black bear. Lake species include grayling. Check state fish and game regulations before fishing. There is no boat.

ASPEN FLATS: The 12- by 14-foot cabin is located in the Kenai Mountains, elevation 600 feet, and is accessible via the Russian Lakes Trail 9 miles from the campground parking area. The cabin sleeps 6 and has a wood stove. Wildlife includes moose and brown and black bear. The upper Russian River offers rainbow trout and Dolly Varden.

UPPER RUSSIAN LAKE: The 12- by 14-foot cabin is located in the Kenai Mountains, elevation 690 feet, and is accessible via the Russian Lakes Trail 12 miles from the campground, or by floatplane 20 minutes from Seward or 20 minutes from Cooper Landing. The cabin sleeps 4 and has a wood stove. Wildlife includes moose and bear. Lake species include rainbow trout. There is a boat for fishing.

UPPER PARADISE LAKE: The 12- by 14-foot cabin is located in the Kenai Mountains, elevation 1,348 feet, and is accessible by floatplane only, 15 minutes from Moose Pass or 25 minutes from Seward. The cabin sleeps 6 and has a wood stove. Wildlife includes goat, moose, and bear. Lake species include grayling. There is a boat for fishing. This is a scenic area.

LOWER PARADISE LAKE: The 12- by 14-foot cabin is located in the Kenai Mountains, elevation 1,199 feet, and is accessible by floatplane only, 15 minutes from Moose Pass or 20 minutes from Seward. The cabin sleeps 6 and has a wood stove. Wildlife includes goat, moose, and bear. Lake species include grayling.

WESTERN
PRINCE WILLIAM SOUND

SOUTH CULROSS PASS: The 12- by 14-foot cabin is located at the southwest end of Culross Pass and is accessible by boat 27 miles from Whittier or by floatplane 45 minutes from Anchorage. The cabin sleeps 6 and has a wood stove. Wildlife includes black bear. There is good crabbing and salmon fishing.

SHRODE LAKE: The 16-foot square cabin is accessible by boat 30 minutes from Whittier or by floatplane 35 minutes from Seward or 45 minutes from Anchorage. The cabin sleeps 10 and has an oil stove. Wildlife includes goat and black bear. Lake species include Dolly Varden. The stream offers salmon. There is a boat for fishing.

PAULSON BAY: The 12- by 14-foot cabin is located on the west side of Cochrane Bay and is accessible by boat 17.5 miles from Whittier or by floatplane 40 minutes from Anchorage. The cabin sleeps 6 and has a wood stove. Wildlife includes black bear. There is good crabbing and salmon fishing.

PIGOT BAY: The 16-foot square cabin is located on the southwest end of Port Wells and is accessible by boat 20 minutes from Whittier or by floatplane 40 minutes from Anchorage. The cabin sleeps 10 and has a wood stove. There is good crabbing and salt- and freshwater salmon fishing.

HARRISON LAGOON: The 16- by 20-foot cabin is located on the west side of Port Wells and is accessible by boat 34 miles from Whittier. The cabin sleeps 5 and has a wood stove. Wildlife includes black bear. There is good crabbing and salmon fishing. You must bring your supply of water.

COGHILL LAKE: The 16-foot square cabin is located at the small lagoon on Coghill Lake in upper Prince William Sound and is accessible by floatplane only, 50 minutes from Anchorage. The cabin sleeps 10 and has a wood stove. Wildlife includes black bear. Lake species include salmon. There is no boat.

INDEX

OTHER BOOKS FROM PACIFIC SEARCH PRESS

COOKING

American Wood Heat Cookery (2d Ed. Revised & Enlarged)
    by Margaret Byrd Adams
The Apple Cookbook by Kyle D. Fulwiler
The Bean Cookbook: Dry Legume Cookery by Norma S. Upson
The Berry Cookbook (2d Ed. Revised & Enlarged)
    by Kyle D. Fulwiler
Canning and Preserving without Sugar (Updated)
    by Norma M. MacRae, R.D.
The Eating Well Cookbook by John Doerper
Eating Well: A Guide to Foods of the Pacific Northwest
    by John Doerper
The Eggplant Cookbook by Norma S. Upson
A Fish Feast by Charlotte Wright
Food 101: A Student Guide to Quick and Easy Cooking
    by Cathy Smith
One Potato, Two Potato: A Cookbook by Constance Bollen
    and Marlene Blessing
River Runners' Recipes by Patricia Chambers
The Salmon Cookbook by Jerry Dennon
Shellfish Cookery: Absolutely Delicious Recipes from the
    West Coast by John Doerper
Starchild & Holahan's Seafood Cookbook by Adam Starchild
    and James Holahan
Wild Mushroom Recipes by Puget Sound Mycological Society
The Zucchini Cookbook (3d Ed. Revised & Enlarged)
    by Paula Simmons

CRAFTS

The Chilkat Dancing Blanket by Cheryl Samuel
The Guide to Successful Tapestry Weaving by Nancy Harvey
An Illustrated Guide to Making Oriental Rugs
    by Gordon W. Scott
Patterns for Tapestry Weaving: Projects and Techniques
    by Nancy Harvey
Spinning and Weaving with Wool (Updated) by Paula Simmons

HEALTH

A Practical Guide to Independent Living for Older People
by Alice H. Phillips and Caryl K. Roman

NATURE

The Birdhouse Book: Building Houses, Feeders, and Baths
by Don McNeil
Growing Organic Vegetables West of the Cascades
by Steve Solomon
Marine Mammals of Eastern North Pacific and Arctic Waters
edited by Delphine Haley
Seabirds of Eastern North Pacific and Arctic Waters
edited by Delphine Haley

NORTHWEST SCENE

At the Forest's Edge: Memoir of a Physician-Naturalist
by David Tirrell Hellyer
The Pike Place Market: People, Politics, and Produce
by Alice Shorett and Murray Morgan
Seattle Photography by David Barnes
They Tried to Cut It All by Edwin Van Syckle

OUTDOOR RECREATION

*Cross-Country Downhill and Other Nordic Mountain Skiing
Techniques* (3d Ed. Revised & Enlarged) by Steve Barnett
The Coastal Kayaker: Kayak Camping on the Alaska and B.C. Coast
by Randel Washburne
Derek C. Hutchinson's Guide to Sea Kayaking
by Derek C. Hutchinson
Kayak Trips in Puget Sound and the San Juan Islands
by Randel Washburne
Kayak Navigation by David Burch
River Runners' Recipes by Patricia Chambers
*The White-Water River Book: A Guide to Techniques,
Equipment, Camping, and Safety*
by Ron Watters/Robert Winslow, photography
*Whitewater Trips for Kayakers, Canoeists, and Rafters in
British Columbia, Greater Vancouver through Whistler
and Thompson River Regions* by Betty Pratt-Johnson
*Whitewater Trips for Kayakers, Canoeists, and Rafters on
Vancouver Island* by Betty Pratt-Johnson

TRAVEL

Alaska's Southeast: Touring the Inside Passage
(2d Ed. Revised & Enlarged) by Sarah Eppenbach
Cruising the Columbia and Snake Rivers (2d Ed. Revised &
Enlarged) by Sharlene P. and Ted W. Nelson and Joan LeMieux
Cruising the Pacific Coast, Acapulco to Skagway
(4th Ed. Revised) by Carolyn and Jack West
The Getaway Guide I: Short Vacations in the Pacific Northwest
(2d Ed. Revised & Enlarged) by Marni and Jake Rankin
The Getaway Guide II: Short Vacations in the Pacific Northwest
(2d Ed. Revised & Enlarged) by Marni and Jake Rankin
The Getaway Guide III: Short Vacations in Northern California
by Marni and Jake Rankin
The Getaway Guide IV: Short Vacations in Southern California
by Marni and Jake Rankin
Journey to the High Southwest: A Traveler's Guide
(2d Ed. Revised) by Robert Casey

PACIFIC SEARCH PRESS will send you books directly if your bookstore does not have what you want!

Quantity	Title	Price	Amount
	ALASKA'S SOUTHEAST: TOURING THE INSIDE PASSAGE, Eppenbach	$11.95	
	JOURNEY TO THE HIGH SOUTHWEST: A TRAVELER'S GUIDE, Casey	$14.95	
	GETAWAY GUIDE I: SHORT VACATIONS IN THE PACIFIC NORTHWEST, Rankin	$ 9.95	
	THE COASTAL KAYAKER: KAYAK CAMPING ON THE ALASKA AND B.C. COAST, Washburne	$10.95	
	Washington State residents add 7.9% sales tax		
	Postage and handling		$ 1.50
	TOTAL ORDER		

☐ Send me a free catalogue of Pacific Search Press titles.

I have enclosed payment of $_____.

I wish to use my credit card.

MasterCard number _____ Expiration date _____

VISA number _____ Expiration date _____

Name _____

Address _____

City _____ State _____ Zip _____

Payment must accompany order.

All orders are sent fourth class book rate. Please allow 3 to 6 weeks for delivery.

SATISFACTION GUARANTEED! If not completely satisfied, return the book(s) to us within 10 days of receipt for a full refund.

PACIFIC SEARCH PRESS
222 Dexter Avenue North
Seattle, Washington 98109
(206) 682-5044